C000155065

SAINTS *alive!*
Life in the Spirit

SAINTS *alive!*

Life in the Spirit

LEADERS MANUAL

JOHN FINNEY AND
FELICITY LAWSON

helping you to help others

Copyright © Anglican Renewal Ministries
1982, 1985, 1990, 1994, 2001

The right of John Finney and Felicity Lawson to be identified
as authors of this work has been asserted by them
in accordance with the
Copyright, Designs and Patents Act 1988.

First published by ARM in 1982
This new edition 2001

All rights reserved.
No part of this publication may be reproduced or
transmitted in any form or by any means, electronic
or mechanical, including photocopy, recording, or any
information storage and retrieval system, without
permission in writing from the publisher.

Unless otherwise indicated, biblical quotations are from
the Good News Bible © American Bible Society 1976,
published by the Bible Society and HarperCollins.

ISBN 1 84291 000 0

Published by
KINGSWAY PUBLICATIONS
Lottbridge Drove, Eastbourne BN23 6NT, England.
Email: books@kingsway.co.uk
in association with
Anglican Renewal Ministries
4 Bramble Street, Derby DE1 1HU
Email: saintsalive@anglican-renewal.org.uk

Cover design and print production for the publishers by
Bookprint Creative Services, P.O. Box 827, BN21 3YJ, England.
Printed in Great Britain.

Contents

Preface

God has been doing exciting and delightful things in his church as the charismatic renewal has become more and more widespread. It started as unusual happenings on the fringe of the church, but has now become the normal Christian experience of millions around the world. It has led to new thinking, new living and new vigour. Indeed it can sometimes be taken for granted. This course was written to make sure that those exploring the Christian faith for the first time or as a refresher were introduced to the Holy Spirit as an essential rather than an optional element of their relationship with God through Jesus Christ. But that is not all: it is important that those who are touched by the Holy Spirit should play their full part as disciples within the church and witnesses within the world.

Since it was first published, *Saints Alive!* has been used by more than 200,000 people of differing denominations in many countries. It has been used in churches which would describe themselves as 'charismatic', but also in many where no such label would be appropriate and where the jargon of 'renewal' would not be appreciated. The basic theology is set out in the Appendix, and the course seeks to lead people into a full-orbed experience of Father, Son and Holy Spirit.

This course was developed when we were working together at a very ordinary church in Nottingham, England. We saw it as vital that the insights of renewal should become part of the normal life and teaching of the local church and be integrated into the tradition of an unexceptional parish church.

The two of us have also had the opportunity of taking about 40 training courses for leaders of Saints Alive! groups, and it is from what these 2,000+ people have taught us that this enlarged edition has come.

The world has not stood still since *Saints Alive!* was first published in 1982. Certain trends and discoveries have been made which affect the church and the world, and have profound implications for leaders of Saints Alive! groups.

- Research shows that relationships are important in people coming to faith – the dynamics of the group and the friendships made are as important as the teaching.

- Research also shows that for the great majority conversion is a journey rather than a one-off event, though there may well be moments of particular significance on that journey.

- Most know less about the Christian faith than previous generations. Many have virtually no knowledge of it. Nothing can be assumed, and the flexibility for which Saints Alive! is renowned is more important than ever. For those coming from a background which has been far from the Christian faith, a new preparatory session has been included which will introduce them to the idea of a relationship with God, and will also give them an opportunity to feel at home in a group.

- Nurture courses such as Saints Alive!, Alpha, Emmaus, Credo and the like have proved to be far and away the most effective tool for evangelism.

- Post-modernism has become as significant as modernism with the result that people are more dependent upon their feelings than their reason, are uneasy about committing themselves to a way of life, and find it difficult to think of anything being 'true'. The implications of this are pointed out in the manual.

The content of the teaching has not been greatly altered in this new edition, but we have introduced a new 'gateway' into the course for those whose experience of the faith is very limited or for those church members who need a different approach.

We have found that leaders need help with the 'mechanics' of leading the course, and the introduction and the explanatory notes have been greatly expanded. We urge course leaders to read the introduction carefully before launching forth. We have retained the video which is central to Session 2, and produced new or revised material which can be used in other sessions.

For us, it has been one of the most fulfilling parts of our ministry to see the joy and surprise in person after person as they come to new life in Christ and begin to take the first steps in ministering to others in the power of the Spirit.

May God use this course to enable many more to come to love Christ and walk in the Spirit.

Felicity Lawson, John Finney
June 2001

Introduction

▶ The aim of this course

The course is intended to give basic teaching on living the Christian life in the power of the Holy Spirit. It offers course members a specific opportunity to respond to Christ and experience his power at work in their own lives.

▶ Structure

The course consists of nine (optionally ten) group meetings, each lasting approximately one-and-a-half hours. There is also 'link-work', which course members are expected to do between group meetings and which is intended to encourage a regular pattern of Bible reading and prayer.

The course has three essential elements:

Teaching

There are teaching outlines and illustrations for each session. They are not intended to be exhaustive, and leaders will need to adapt the notes in ways which are appropriate to each group.

The course does not pretend that it can convey the whole expanse of Christian teaching in nine weeks, but it provides basic teaching and an opportunity for ministry, and gives course members a hunger to explore further into the immense richness of the faith.

Ministry

Ministry has been defined as 'one Christian acting in love to another person'. But there needs also to be specific opportunities when people are invited to respond to God. Suggestions as to when it might be appropriate to offer ministry to group members are given throughout the course. There are also hints as to how this might be done, but a reliance upon the guidance of the Holy Spirit is indispensable. Opportunities for ministry should be taken whenever it seems right, but the invitation to receive ministry in Session 6 should always be made.

Fellowship

When those who have been on a nurture course are asked what they valued most, the usual answer is 'meeting people'. To be in a group where confidentialities are kept, love is shown and they experience the work of Christ together, is a new adventure for most participants. This means that the chatter before and after sessions is almost as important a part of the course as the more structured times for discussion. Space should be left for this informality (possibly aided by a meal or refreshments).

▶ The shape of the course

Life in the Spirit focuses on the Trinity and the life of the church. A glance at the contents will show that:

- **Session 1** looks at the being of God our Father and our need for a relationship with him.
- **Sessions 2 and 3** look at the life, death and resurrection of Jesus Christ.
- **Sessions 4 and 5** concentrate on the work of the Holy Spirit.
- **Session 6** gives an opportunity for course members to respond to what they have learned and experienced of God.
- **Sessions 7 to 9** look at the life of the Christian disciple – prayer, Bible reading, sacraments and commitment to the local church.

(The biblical basis for this Trinitarian approach is outlined in the Appendix.)

▶ Who is the course for?

Those who mean business! Anyone who wants to know more of God's love and power in their own life and is prepared to do something about it will find the course helpful. Previous Christian knowledge is unimportant but a yearning to explore is essential.

Four types of people may be found in a Saints Alive! group.

- **Enquirers:** those who have been contacted through visiting, baptism and marriage preparation, Sunday school parents and so on. These may well have very little Christian background and have just become curious about the Christian faith and want to know more without any further commitment.

- **Young Christians:** those who have recently come to faith. They will often be candidates for confirmation, adult baptism and so on.

- **New church members:** those who have recently joined the congregation from another church. The course gives them an opportunity to get to know the leaders of the church and some of the members of the congregation at a far deeper level than if they just came to Sunday services, and helps them to find out what makes their new church tick spiritually. It also means that the leaders of the church get to know the new members on a spiritual as well as a social level.

- **Christians needing a refresher:** members of the congregation who want to have a 'refresher' course in order to think through their faith at their present stage in life or to explore the work of the Holy Spirit. Often they still need to ask very basic questions and may be embarrassed by their ignorance after so many years of church membership. For them, the presence of non-Christians and very untutored Christians in the group can be of real help. Do not skip material because it is thought to be too 'elementary' for such people.

Above all, the leadership of the church should be praying that the right people come on each course. Then leaders will know that the people in the group have been handpicked by God, and it can be assumed that he intends each person to change and grow spiritually. This knowledge that 'all are called and none called for no purpose' will give confidence for ministry.

Opt in

It has been found that course members need to 'opt in' to the group, rather than Saints Alive! being introduced as part of the normal programme for an existing group. Hence it is not always appropriate for a house group unless all the members are really trying to come closer to God.

Age of course members

In most churches a Saints Alive! group will have people from a wide range of ages and backgrounds. Far from being a problem, this has been found to be positively enriching as course members encourage and learn from each other, the Holy Spirit interpreting the teaching to each person at their point of need. Although Saints Alive! is primarily for adults, older teenagers (15+) both appreciate and contribute much to a group. Some churches have adapted the course successfully for groups of 11- to 15-year-olds.

Size of the group

It has been found that the best groups consist of about nine members, plus two leaders, plus (possibly) two assistant leaders. Much larger groups have been used at times but it has proved difficult to give the personal care and teaching which each individual requires. Where larger groups are unavoidable, the material should be presented in such a way that there are opportunities for smaller groups to be formed from time to time in order that the inarticulate can talk, the retiring can become known and the burning questions be voiced.

It is common for the first course or two to be fairly large and composed mainly of church members. As confidence in Saints Alive! grows, church members ask their non-Christian friends to come. Later courses therefore have a drop in numbers but a rise in evangelistic effectiveness. Research shows that only after a nurture course has been run three times does it lead to church growth.

FLEXIBILITY

Saints Alive! Life in the Spirit is there to be your servant – you can change it, adapt it, make it your own. Many leaders find that after running it a few times, they hardly need to look at the book.

The course is flexible enough to be used with different kinds of groups in a variety of settings, and leaders will need wisdom in adapting it to each situation. It has been used in prisons and in universities, in Two-Thirds World as well as in First World contexts. It has been used in groups where no one apart from the leaders were Christians and also in groups where all were ordained ministers.

▶ How can the course be used?

Although the course can be used as a 'one-off', it has been found to be most useful if it is run regularly as part of the church programme. The church where it began used it three times each year to coincide with school terms. Other churches have used it virtually continuously, using the members of one group to recruit the next. (Some suggestions about this are given in the notes in Session 9.)

It has been found that it is generally unwise to lengthen the course by putting in extra sessions or making one session cover more than one meeting. While this may be right occasionally for a group which is making heavy weather of a particular piece of teaching, a course like this has a certain 'pace'. If it is too drawn out, it loses momentum. For the same reason it is best if there is one session each week. While occasional breaks may be inevitable, if the course is spread over too long a time pace is lost and members are unable to hold in their memory all that has been taught and too much time is spent on recapitulation. On the other hand, those churches which have tried to cover the material in a three-day conference have found that members have suffered 'information overload' and have been unable to benefit fully.

Whatever pattern of meetings is chosen, the opportunity for ministry in Session 6 should always be included.

▶ What happens when the course is finished?

People are never the same after they have been through a Saints Alive! course. Now, more than ever, they will need to be integrated into the church fellowship and encouraged to go on growing and serving as Christians. Careful thought needs to be given to this before a course is planned.

If the congregation has a house-group structure, then it is possible either:

● to feed people from the course into different existing groups;
● or to keep the group together.

In practice, the latter has been found to be more successful. Every group develops its own very marked identity and forms a network of trusting and caring relationships. Members do not find it easy to transfer from the 'relaxed warmth' of a group they know and among whom they have found Christ to a group of 'threatening strangers' (however welcoming they are)! If it is decided that the course might continue as a group, then co-leaders, who will become the leaders of the new group, should be included from the start so that they can build relationships with course members.

Much of the material in the Emmaus 'Growth' books (written by a group which includes the two authors of *Life in the Spirit* and published by CHP) is particularly appropriate. It is specifically designed for a group which has been through a nurture course.

If the church has a central mid-week meeting rather than groups, then it is important that mature Christians are encouraged to befriend course members and, once the course is finished, to accompany them to meetings and generally exercise pastoral oversight. These 'sponsors' should not be the course leaders, for it has to be recognised that those who are leading more than one Saints Alive! course cannot provide friendship and care to an ever-increasing number of people.

It is pastorally disastrous if those who have found Christ through a Saints Alive! course are left unprayed for and uncared for to flounder unaided in the (icy?) waters of the church swimming pool.

▶ Leadership

As in every other area of the church's life, leadership is vital. Good leadership which takes full advantage of the in-built flexibility of the course will enable members to receive the maximum benefit and spiritual growth.

Mature (which does not mean old!) leadership is necessary on several counts:

- The notes given for each session presuppose a certain amount of biblical, spiritual and theological understanding on the part of the leaders. The course encourages participation by all members, and leaders have to be prepared to explain Christian truth in a way which provokes discussion. They should not be frightened of the unexpected question and be able to pick up the insights of others.

- The course makes considerable spiritual demands on the leaders as they seek to love the members, to help them in times of confusion and to minister to them in the power of the Spirit.

- The course draws on the Christian experience of the leaders. It is not a course about the theory of the Christian life, but about living it in the power of the Holy Spirit. We cannot lead people where we have not been ourselves.

- A course like this requires the leaders to be able to teach adults, and to be responsive to the differing needs of each group. It does not need a degree in educational theory, but each session needs decisions on how material will be presented, what else is required, how visual aids are best used, etc.

- We are praying that each person undertaking a course of this kind will change: they are therefore very vulnerable as they come under the work of the Holy Spirit. This requires sensitivity and care on the part of the leaders, who need to be aware of what God is doing in each person and respond accordingly. 'Leadership is an expression of love.'

Training and support for leaders

Leaders should be encouraged to receive training wherever possible. Probably the best training is to act as an assistant leader to experienced leaders who have already been used by God in this ministry. Books and courses on Christian adult education will also be found useful. Churches should ensure that their Saints Alive! leaders receive as much help as possible, for these groups spearhead the evangelism of the church.

> In the Bible leadership is linked with 'diligence' (see Romans 12:8).

However, we need to remember that our ideal is that 'we do not speak in words taught by human wisdom but in words taught by the Spirit' (1 Corinthians 2:13). The success of the course does not depend upon skill in group dynamics or counselling, however valuable these may be, but upon our ability to hear the voice of the Spirit and to allow him to speak through us to those on the course. Prayer for each course member and for ourselves as leaders is vital and should never be neglected.

The leadership of a Saints Alive! group requires a high degree of commitment, is very taxing spiritually, and demands much time. It is much more exacting than running a house group. If leaders are undertaking this regularly it is important that they are relieved of other work in the church and that they are supported by persistent prayer and encouragement.

Number of leaders

It is strongly advised that at least two leaders take each group. This provides mutual support, differences of style and teaching gifts, greater availability for pastoral care of group members and a biblical model of Christian leadership. It has been found helpful if the minister or someone in senior leadership in the church helps to lead one or two courses when they are first introduced. However, courses are demanding of time and energy and it is probably best if they train others to take over the leadership as soon as possible. Where possible it has been found valuable if the leaders differ from each other: e.g. clergy/laity; men/women; younger/older. It should be remembered that the course includes a 'one-to-one meeting' with each course member as well as ministry and teaching within the group, and the pastoral sensitivity which that requires.

If it is envisaged that the course will continue as a group, then assistant leaders need to be included from the beginning. They can be introduced as such at the first meeting and included, as appropriate, in the planning, teaching and time of ministry. If it is likely that more than about 15 people will be taking the course on any one occasion, then it is important to appoint assistant leaders (regardless of the future of the group) who will be able to lead small group discussions and so on.

▶ Preparation

Leaders should have a meeting between each of the course meetings.

Agenda

1 Review of the last session: what went well, what could be improved, who was struggling etc.

2 Preparation of the next session: what sections need expanding or cutting, who leads each section, who is responsible for visual aids.

3 Prayer for those on the course.

4 Mutual support and encouragement.

Experience shows that flexibility of approach comes from knowing the material very well indeed. This gives the confidence to depart from it when necessary or to present it in a different order than that set out in the manual.

This Saints Alive! manual is spiral bound so that it can readily sit on your knee or a nearby table during a session. Try to avoid having too many pieces of paper – write brief notes in your manual and/or have one piece of paper to refer to.

▶ Presentation

The course is designed to last for nine sessions, each of about one-and-a-half hours. The concurrent course of 'link-work' consists of daily Bible readings and an extended 'chunk reading' of Mark and Acts. This is to be found in the booklet that accompanies the course (obtainable from your local Christian bookshop or from Anglican Renewal Ministries). The link-work ceases after Session 7 so that regular Bible reading notes can be introduced.

Worship

Each session should normally begin with prayer for the session. Closing worship should be relaxed and prolonged if it seems right (sing if you have the resources and group members are familiar with the songs – but beware of a Christian singalong). Members of the group should be invited to participate as soon as possible, by bidding prayers, one-sentence thanksgivings, prayers written before the meeting. Above all the prayer time should be kept simple and open to the Holy Spirit. One-word prayers can help people get used to the sound of their own voice, e.g. 'Let us pray for the sick...' ('Mary', 'Jack') or 'Let us praise God through remembering some of his names...' ('Emmanuel', 'Redeemer', 'Good Shepherd'). The leaders should pray that as the course continues the gifts of the Spirit may be exercised, but this should not be forced.

Our task is to help people to relax and feel comfortable, not to make them embarrassed. If new ideas are introduced, worship should flow from the familiar to the unfamiliar.

Food

Research shows that Christian friendship and fellowship have been a very important factor in people coming to faith. Food and drink has its part in this, either before or after sessions. It helps people to relax and can be a time for laughter and discovery, which lays the foundation of those vital friendships upon which so much depends. In most social contexts a buffet type meal is better than sitting more formally round the table, as people can mix more easily (it is also easier for course members to bring food they have provided). A meal together can be a regular practice unless:

- you do not have the facilities to do it and the people to prepare it (which should not normally be the course leaders);
- it causes domestic friction for course members – a seething wife left at home to put the children to bed is not going to hear the gospel her husband tells her;
- meals together are not part of the normal social context (dinner parties are common in some areas, while in others no one outside the family is invited over the doorstep);
- the food becomes a distraction from the main purpose of the session.

Different Saints Alive! groups have had varying experiences in regard to food, and there are no general rules (except that refreshments or a meal should be served at Session 1, and a meal as part of Session 9 is always valuable).

Tea/coffee/biscuits at the end of the sessions may be all that is needed to help course members to relax and get to know one another.

Where to meet

The nature of the meeting place has a big influence on the group. The relaxed atmosphere of a home is preferable to a draughty church hall. Remember that a video will be required for certain sessions. Frequently the home of one of the leaders will be used. The homes of course members can be used, but sometimes this can mean they are more concerned with providing refreshments at the right time than with Christian truth.

Visual aids

Some visual aids need preparing beforehand, but generally it is best if a picture is built up while teaching is being given. It is better to draw, however badly, as you talk, than to have it produced neatly in advance. Sometimes an outline can be sketched beforehand which is then filled in. It is preferable to draw on a piece of paper attached to a clipboard or on the floor than to stand by the wall in true 'teacher' fashion.

We live in a visual age and can become obsessed by overelaborate visual aids. The best visual aids are the leaders themselves, if their faces are alight with their enthusiasm for Christ and their concern for the course members shows.

The group members: who are they?

Before the course begins, think and pray for each member, bearing in mind the following questions:

- **What is the Christian background of each person?**
  Can they find their way through the Bible? Do they think you get to heaven by manning a stall at the summer fête? Even life-long church members may have some very strange ideas and need to ask some very basic questions. You will need to move at the speed of the slowest ship in the convoy, and blessed indeed is that group with a member who is of such simplicity of soul that they ask the questions everyone else wants to ask but dare not.

- **Why did each member join the course?**
  Their conscious needs will emerge as you meet together, but leaders also need to listen to the Lord for insight about what are the real reasons.

- **What is their educational background?**
  Remember:
  ~ Over 50 per cent of the population never read a book, and certainly not one as big as the Bible.
  ~ We live in a TV age and most folk are not used to listening to lectures; seek for variety of presentation and use plenty of visual aids and personal testimony.
  ~ Most people have not had tertiary education.
  ~ We live in the person-centred age of post-modernism rather than the modernist age of words and ideas.

The presentation of each session should be influenced by the way in which the questions above are answered.

To help leaders there are two possible 'routes' which can be followed in the first vital session.

If you find that the majority of the group have very little knowledge of the faith and may not be ready to embark immediately on a discussion about God, a preparatory session may be useful. Furthermore, if you find that members are not used to being in a group which talks about spiritual and emotionally charged issues, you may find an 'ice-breaker' session would be helpful (this may be true of church members as well as non-churchgoers). Route A is designed for people from this background.

Route A starts with two sessions:

Session 1a
A preparatory session looking at issues surrounding human identity in which all can take part. It also pays particular attention to the dynamics of the group. This session ends with a brief introduction to the idea of a relationship with God.

Session 1b
This shows our need for a relationship with God and introduces the person of Jesus Christ.

Route B may be more appropriate for those who have some knowledge of the faith and some experience of working in a group. It has only one session, which deals in more traditional language with sin and salvation, and how God has taken the initiative in seeking us in Christ.

▶ The course video

The video has a variety of material which can be used in different sessions. With the exception of 'The Message of the Cross' in Session 2, use of the video should be seen as entirely optional. Leaders should view the video carefully before the course begins so that they can pick out those sections they wish to use.

'The Cottage', 'Evidence for the resurrection' and 'Gifts of the Spirit' are intended to give a different face and voice for some of the longer passages of straight teaching. Using them may have the added benefit of facilitating discussion on new or controversial areas as it may be easier to question teaching on a video than that offered by a course leader. The testimonies can be used to supplement those available within the group.

The precise timing of each session can be found on the video inlay.

Contents

Leading the course Brief reflections from leaders. Can be used at preparatory meeting for course leaders and/or at Church Council.

Introductory meeting Course members say how they came to join the course.

Route A Session la or **Route B(1)** Welcome to the Course: John Finney and Felicity Lawson introduce the course.

Route A Session lb or **Route B(1)** The Cottage: Felicity Lawson gives the illustration from Section D.

Session 2 The Message of the Cross: An illustrated account of the Passion narrated by Chris Lane.

Session 3 Evidence for the Resurrection: Felicity Lawson explores teaching given in Section C(i).

Session 4 Personal Experience of the Holy Spirit: Course members share their experience following the laying on of hands.

Session 5a The Gifts of the Spirit: John Finney introduces the teaching in Section C.

Session 5b Using the Gifts: Examples from personal experience.

Session 8 After the Course: Course members share their experiences.

LEADER'S CHECKLIST

An agenda of what needs to be done before you start:

◆ Talk over the proposed course with the leadership of the church – minister, church council etc. If Saints Alive! is being used for the first time, consider using the relevant parts of the video and/or invite someone from another church which has used this course to speak of their experience. Ensure a church leader is available for the introductory meeting.

◆ Decide when and where the course will meet. A certain flexibility in dates and places may be helpful until the introductory meeting when course members can discuss which day will suit them best.

◆ Arrange a meeting for leaders before the introductory meeting in order to 'pray in' the course members and to go through the course in outline, so that an overview is gained. It will be helpful to watch the video and to see how the elements within it can best be used. Decide which of the 'Routes' for the first session you are going to follow.

◆ Decide what will happen to course members once the course ends. Do you need to select and prepare assistant leaders? Do you need to begin to look for course material?

◆ Publicise the introductory meeting (see below) and begin prayerfully suggesting to people that they might like to think about joining the course. Publicity should be wide-spread so that anyone is free to join, and there is no suspicion of a 'hole-in-the-corner' group being formed. There should be some way in which prospective members can show their interest (for example, a response slip or a list at the back of church). This helps them to begin the process of commitment and enables you to know the numbers that will be involved. In some churches it may be right to invite people to come to the introductory meeting and only ask for a definite response after that. (For ideas on how to attract people from outside the church look at the *Contact* booklet in the Emmaus material or look at a book like *50 Simple Outreach Ideas* by Paul Mogford, Kingsway 1999.)

◆ Purchase sufficient copies of the Link-work book from your local Christian bookshop. If the group has people who are non-literate, the provision of audio tapes with recordings of Mark's Gospel and Acts should be considered.

◆ Purchase the course video and ensure that a video is available for the sessions when you will be using it.

◆ Put dates in your diaries for preparation meetings between the sessions.

◆ Decide on the version of the Bible you wish to use – it is a great help if all use the same version with the same page numbers. The *Good News Bible* has been found to be particularly suitable for those with little Christian background and the link-work daily readings have been based upon it. (Remember that course members are being asked to read large chunks of the Bible, so a modern version is helpful.)

◆ If food is being provided, decide how this is going to happen and who is to be responsible.

◆ Decide if you will give course members Link-work books, or whether you will encourage them to buy them (the same question may arise with Bibles and Bible reading notes). Often people value most what they have paid for.

Introductory meeting

This meeting may only take 30–45 minutes, perhaps after a service in church, but it is *essential*, both to sort out the practical details and also to set the 'tone' of the course. Prospective members should be encouraged to make every effort to attend.

It has been found that a mood of 'happy determination' should prevail at this meeting, without it being heavy. Joining the course should be seen to be a serious undertaking, so the challenge to do regular link-work and attend regularly should not be underplayed, but a friendly atmosphere of mutual exploration should prevail. A little light-hearted banter is helpful, for those from outside the church may well expect long faces and solemnity.

Administrative arrangements should be carefully prepared – it shows that the leaders are careful and sensible. Uncertainty increases nervousness.

Someone from the church leadership should chair the meeting and introduce the other leaders. The following points should be made:

- **The course is for beginners not experts.** We will be starting at the beginning and will not be shocked by ignorance or questions about the existence of God and so on.

- During this nine-week course (ten weeks if Route A is followed) we shall look at the work of God our Father and how he sent his Son, Jesus, and the Holy Spirit into the world. However, we shall not just be looking backwards at what happened two thousand years ago, but at what these events mean for us today. We shall be seeing again and again how these can make a difference in our everyday lives. **We shall also be looking for God to touch each of our lives in different ways and there will be times when we can open ourselves to him if we wish.**

- **The course will mean different things to each person**, because we all come with different needs. Some will know more about God than others. However, we are expecting each person to come closer to Christ during the course and to discover more of his will for their lives. **All on the course, including the leaders, will experience change as God works in our lives.**

- **The course demands commitment** of a fairly high standard in setting aside time for the course as an absolute priority, doing the link-work and being prepared actively to seek God.

- **Each session will last for 90 minutes** and there will always be a break after 90 minutes *(for those who are being picked up or have to catch a bus)*.

- **If someone wants to drop out of the course** at any point that is fine. *(Don't hassle them, but it would be helpful if they were to let you know so that you do not think they are ill.)*

- Course members usually get to know one another quite well during a course, and this is one of its perks. However, **it is quite all right to come along and sit at the back and say nothing.** *(Do not worry – they will not actually stay quiet for very long, but some may be extremely apprehensive at what might be demanded of them in terms of participation!)* **All discussion will be helpful** and there will be plenty of opportunities for asking questions, **but argument for argument's sake will harm the group**.

- To make for a free discussion it will be expected that all members will **keep things they learn in the group about other people confidential** – though what they learn about the Christian faith they can talk about with anyone! *(They may need reminding about confidentiality at other times in the course – and the leaders should set an example!)*

- Members will need to purchase a copy of the **Link-work book** *(if this has been decided upon – see 'Leader's checklist' above)* and **a notebook**, and to bring **a Bible**. It is helpful if all members have the same version, and better still the same edition, so that you can refer to pages rather than to chapter and verse.

- If it is intended that the group should continue as a group after the course is finished, **introduce the assistant leaders** and briefly outline future possibilities. Explain that there will be no compulsion on anyone to join any continuing group.

- **Arrange the date, place and time of at least the first three meetings**. Suggest that members might like to help one another with transport. (This begins to build relationships and also helps those who will find actually getting to the first session a nerve-racking business, especially if it is held in a big house. A written reminder of time and place a few days before the first meeting will also help.)

- Ask the group to **begin praying for one another** and for the leaders between now and the beginning of the course. Remind them that they are not the only person feeling rather nervous.

- **Any questions?** The video 'Introductory meeting' can be shown. The video 'Session 1a: Welcome to the Course' could also be used here instead of in Session 1.

1a Preparatory session

> Notes before starting the preparatory session:
>
> ◆ If you have not yet read the Introduction, please do so before embarking on this session – it is very important.
>
> ◆ In the text, the basic teaching outline is given in normal serif type, while the ideas for the presentation are given in plain type (like this text) following an arrow ➜.
>
> ◆ It is assumed that the introductory meeting has been held before this session.

(Some parts of these notes on Session 1a apply to every session and are not repeated later.)

Aims

◆ To enable those unused to working in a group to feel at ease in discussing religious and ethical questions, and to encourage them to contribute.

◆ To help those with little knowledge of the faith to come to see the importance of relationships – with themselves, with others and with God.

◆ To be a preparation for Session 1b.

(While this session has been prepared primarily for those who are unfamiliar with the church, it may also be helpful for church members, especially if they have not been used to meeting in a group situation.)

Leading the session

In this session establishing healthy dynamics in the group is as important as the teaching given. The introductions, the discussion between group members and the relaxed meal or refreshments are most important (guidance is given on this in the Introduction p. 10). Fun and lightheartedness are to be encouraged wherever appropriate.

To help in this process, the emotions which are present should be brought to the surface and acknowledged, though not too much time should be spent exploring them. Many members will be greatly reassured if they learn that they are not the only ones who:

- are feeling nervous and frightened that they will be put into toe-curlingly embarrassing situations;
- are not sure that there is a God;
- are highly cynical about the institution (the church);
- think that churchgoers are a hypocritical bunch;
- are vaguely interested in spiritual things but do not see what the church has to do with spirituality;
- at best think the Bible is full of 'nice stories', at worst regard it as incomprehensible;
- fear that if they get 'religious', they will be isolated from their families and friends.

(These attitudes have been identified in research done by David Hay and Kate Hunt into the spirituality of the non-churched. Obviously not everyone in your group will have all these opinions, but some of these attitudes will almost certainly be present, even among church-goers.)

It is a help if the leaders acknowledge publicly their own feelings – it is unusual not to feel nervous and inadequate when first meeting a group. However, do not overdo it or group members will think the leaders are incompetent and they need to sense that someone is in control!

The teaching is intended to be straightforward enough to enable non-Christians to have as much to offer as those who have been Christians for years. Everyone can speak about their own experience of life and their relationships with those around them. At the same time no one should be put in a position where they are made to speak – fear of making a fool of oneself is very near the surface in this session.

The matters discussed may be profound but the content of the session should be easy to follow, thus the only passages of Scripture used are likely to be well known – though the thoughts which flow from them may not be. The temptation to expand this with more teaching should be resisted. The more the members of the group talk the better, so the leaders should say as little as possible. This requires self-discipline, for if we are nervous we tend to talk too much.

This session looks at three relationships:
- with ourselves;
- with others;
- (briefly) with God.

Session 1b) looks in much more detail into the relationship between us and God, so this preparatory session looks primarily at the first two. The temptation to move too quickly to God should be resisted – in this session anyway!

The idea of God requiring us to love ourselves may well be a new and enlightening one to many, and should not be skated over. There may well be some who think that God requires us to be masochists (which is not the meaning of Christ's words about 'denying' ourselves).

Further the revolutionary command to 'love your neighbour' – who may be your enemy – should not be rushed. If people leave with a sense of the excitement and radical nature of Christian living and the support it can give to themselves, a firm foundation has been laid for the teaching about the relationship with God which is considered in Session 1b. The image of God lurking in people's minds may be that of a stern headmaster rather than one who delights in love and laughter.

The introductory meeting will have given members some idea of what is involved but this may well need repeating (especially the administrative details concerning the meetings). Certainly space should be given for them to ask any questions they may have about the arrangements.

 Timing

Timing is given throughout the course in order to give an indication of the way in which the session could be spaced. However, it should never be kept to rigidly, and a great degree of flexibility should be used. This is especially true in this preparatory session where one of the main aims is to establish the dynamics of the group and encourage as many as possible to take part. However, the total time of 90 minutes should be kept to, particularly at this first session where the pattern for the future is set.

0–20 mins	Prayer and A Introductions
20–25	B The triangle of love
25–40	C Loving ourselves
40–70	D Friends and enemies
70–87	E Us and God
87–90	G Prayer

It is good practice to put alongside your notes (or in this book) the time you intend to take for each section – not as a straitjacket but as a guide.

Presentation

It is assumed that there have been refreshments before this session, during which group members have begun to relax and to get to know each other.

Even though the practice may well be unfamiliar to some, it is wise to begin with a *brief* prayer to underline the Godward aspect of the course. The exception may be when the preceding refreshments have gone with such a swing that it is natural to proceed directly to the introductions in Section A without a break.

A Introductions

In this session, this section is not just a preliminary to get through before getting down to the real business, but one of its most important elements. If they are strangers to each other, the members of the group are not going to be able to remember the names and faces of everyone – it is better that they get to know two or three others. (The time-honoured method of going round the group and asking everyone to say something about themselves can be terrifying for some and is best avoided.)

The leaders should begin by introducing themselves to the group (even if this has been done at the introductory meeting – there was a great deal of information given at the meeting and names get forgotten).

There are a large number of 'introduction games' which can be played. If leaders know one which would be suitable, by all means use that, rather than the one suggested here. However, make sure that:

● people are not put in an embarrassing situation;
● it is not assumed that people can read aloud, or are confident enough to speak in a new situation (like the group);
● the game does not become an end in itself, or take too long;
● it is appropriate to the number of people you have and the size of the room you are meeting in;
● it does not assume any particular knowledge (e.g. of the Bible).

→ SUGGESTED 'INTRODUCTION GAME'

Give everyone a piece of A4 paper folded into four, and a pen/pencil. Ask each person to put:
● in the top left-hand corner – a picture or description of their favourite animal;
● in the top right-hand corner – their favourite colour;
● in the bottom left-hand corner – the name of someone they admire (dead or alive);
● in the bottom right-hand corner – the title of a book, film or TV programme which has meant a lot to them.

Ask them to discuss their choices with two people near them.

However, an introductory game is not essential. For example, you can simply gather people in triplets and ask them to say something about themselves to the other two.

Once the introductions have been made let the members voice their feelings. They may well arise naturally from the introductions but you can ask with a smile, 'What are you feeling?' The responses may well be those set out above in 'Leading the session'.

Acknowledge these views but do not spend too much time on them. It is a help to the group simply to know that others feel the same as themselves. It also gives them a chance to talk about their feelings.

→ If you wish, show the video 'Session 1a: Welcome to the Course'.

B The triangle of love

We relate to:

- ● ourselves
- ● other people
- ● God

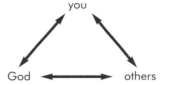

→ (If required this diagram can be photocopied or scanned and enlarged but it is probably best drawn freehand.)

Give each person a paper or card with the following:

The commandments of love 'Love the Lord your God... Love your neighbour as you love yourself.' (Mark 12:30,31)	(As you give this out you might wish to point out that the Bible is divided into books, chapters and verses for easy reference – and that there is an index at the beginning.)

We shall be looking at these in reverse order.

C Loving ourselves

Many people find it difficult to make a sound relationship with themselves, yet it is very important that we do. If we lack self-respect, or hate what we are, we shall be limited people. More than that we shall think, 'If that is what I think about myself, what do other people think about me?'

Ask the group to make two lists side by side. One list sets out the terms we may use when we feel good about ourselves, the other the negative terms we may use.

→ The leader (or a volunteer) writes the results with a felt-tip pen on a large sheet of paper (kneeling and crawling on the floor helps to relax the group, who may be sitting rather stiffly on chairs). Alternatively, write on A4 pages and toss them on the floor. Answers might include:

Positive	Negative
content	shame
on top of things	lacking in confidence
peaceful, etc	dislike of oneself, etc

Mention, without elaboration, that later we shall be looking at the fact that allowing ourselves to be loved unconditionally by God helps us to love ourselves. We become part of God's family and he is our Father in heaven (as the Lord's Prayer says).

Discuss with the group: 'If we have a right love of ourselves, how can it affect our actions and our feelings? What is the effect if we do not love ourselves?'

Almost certainly someone will mention the fact that our view of ourselves affects the way we relate to other people, which leads naturally into the next section.

D Friends and enemies

Human beings are social creatures. We are born into a family, join the community of a school and the great majority work with other people. We socialise with others in shops and pubs and football matches. Some of us attend endless 'meetings'. We have a web of relationships.

➔ On a large piece of paper on the floor, sketch out a 'spider', with oneself (or a volunteer) represented by a fairly small circle in the middle and then lines stretching out to the different areas of one's life where one encounters other people – home, church, work, leisure activities, Internet chat rooms, shops, etc.

We look for acceptance from others and we have within us that which longs to be accepted by other people.

➔ Retell Luke 10:29–37 briefly in your own words.

Christ told us to love our neighbour. The famous story of the good Samaritan showed us that everyone is our neighbour. The Samaritan was divided from the wounded man by religion, race and locality, let alone the threat of attack upon himself and the trouble and cost which he incurred. Yet he stretched out his hand when others who claimed to be religious hurried past.

Jesus also said something which he recognised at the time was radical in the extreme: 'You have heard that it was said, "You shall love your neighbour and hate your enemy." But I say to you, "Love your enemies and pray for those who persecute you"' (Matthew 5:43–44 RSV).

People have been trying to come to terms with that ever since. If you know of a suitable story which illustrates love of one's enemy, not necessarily from a Christian source, this would be a good finale to this section.

E Us and God

Next week we shall be looking in more detail into this area.

Think about these two ideas so that we can discuss them next week. *(Produce them on a card/ sheet of paper for members to take away.)*

Do not explain – seed thoughts need time to germinate.

> Seed thoughts
>
> 1. Love which is not prepared to suffer is not love.
>
> 2. We cannot earn love.

🇫 Link-work

Leave the distribution of Link-work books until Session 1b. If the preliminary session has achieved its aim they will have a lot to think about, both in terms of the social connections they have made and the new ideas they have been introduced to.

🇬 Prayer

If this group consists of non-churchgoers, be very sensitive at this time. It may be that a brief thanksgiving prayer is all that is required, coupled with bringing before God any personal needs which have surfaced during the meeting. It is unlikely that with such a group the singing of unfamiliar songs is appropriate (even if there are some church people present who know them).

🇭 Refreshments

Encourage the group to stay and chat. Have refreshments if they have not been provided at the beginning.

1b We meet God

Aims

◆ To explore the relationship between us and God so that it is brought into the centre of the picture, where it will remain for the rest of the course.

◆ To show how God took the initiative in sending his Son, and so lay the foundation for Session 2.

Leading the session

Session 1a should have begun the process of forming a group of friends going on an exploration together. They will have begun to relax in each other's company and it will be becoming plain who are the noisy and the shy, the opinionated and the receptive, the comic and the serious. In this session there may still be a need for introductions (for it is unlikely they will have remembered each other's names). The group may need some time to recapture the freedom of discussion they might have found in the previous session and the introductory conversations should not be rushed. A short ice-breaker may be useful.

Section B is optional. There may be some who doubt the existence of God and wish to talk it through. Suggestions are made as to how this may be handled. Other groups may not regard this as an issue and be bored by the subject. As a rule of thumb, deal with it if it arises from the group, but do not raise the subject if it doesn't.

Every session begins with the present experience of the group members. Thus this session begins with an examination of parent–child relationships, with which both Christians and non-Christians can identify and have something to contribute to the discussion.

There is then a section drawing out the meaning of love – its reality is shown by a person's willingness to suffer for the one they love. This introduces the idea of the incarnation and the suffering of Christ which is drawn out further in Session 2.

At the end of the session the link-work books are introduced and given out. Spend time on this, particularly stressing that this is for their own benefit and the books will not be 'collected in' or 'marked': the last time this sort of thing may have happened to group members may be the giving out of exercise books in school.

 Timing

The timing will have to be adjusted in those groups which wish to look at Section B on the existence of God.

0–35 mins	Prayer and A Recap
[10–30	B The existence of God (optional)]
30–65	C The parenthood of God
65–70	D Illustration
70–80	E Link-work
80–90	F Prayer

▪️ Presentation

→ It is likely that members will now feel more at ease and will have the confidence to bring up matters which have been troubling them, even if they are not relevant to the aim of this session. They may have been bottling them up for years. If a member raises a point which is strictly personal or intellectually beyond the range of the rest of the group, arrange to see them privately.

Begin the session with prayer. It may be right to introduce the prayer with a period of silence in which the members of the group are encouraged to calm their thoughts and ask for God's help for each other in the session. (Different methods of prayer can be introduced by way of example throughout the course.)

A Recap

Remind them of the two sentences they were given in the last session:

1 Love which is not prepared to suffer is not love.

2 We cannot earn love.

Ask them if they have had any ideas about these seed thoughts during the past week.

→ Develop these ideas without spending too much time on them, unless their response comes from personal experience. It is more important that a fair number of people speak than that particularly profound ideas surface.

God is a person and therefore we can have a relationship with him. He is not a thing, an 'it', but has personality – it would, after all, be rather strange if the Creator of the whole universe had no more identity than a stone, and less than ourselves whom he created.

→ Do not assume that your concept of God is the same as that of the group members. Some of them may see 'God' as:
- all of creation – a nature god;
- an old-man-in-the-sky – either benign or punitive;
- a force for good in the world;
- a spirit – as conceived in much New Age thinking;
- 'something out there which has influence over my life' e.g. through the stars, crystals, extra-terrestrials etc.

If these sorts of views about 'spirituality' are voiced by members of the group, do not condemn them, but suggest that we are exploring what Jesus can teach us and we shall see if our ideas develop.

B The existence of God (optional)

→ It may be unnecessary to raise the issue of whether God exists or not if the members of the group already believe in his existence. However, if it is a matter of deep personal concern to members, then spend time on this but avoid an intellectual discussion which will divert you from the purpose of the session.

➔ There may be some who doubt the existence of God. If so, this needs to be thought through. One way of doing this would be to explore with the group possible grounds for belief, drawing these out of group members where possible.

It may be helpful to remind the group of the sheer scale and wonder of the universe – from the sub-atomic particles of extraordinary diversity to the billions of stars which shine in the sky. However, avoid subjects like life on other planets, extra-terrestrial beings, the Gaia hypothesis and similar speculations which many find fascinating.

God is, by his very nature, a relationship – Father, Son and Holy Spirit. He is also the source of love. And relationships and love cannot be 'proved' in a scientific way, yet they are some of the most important elements within our lives, making us happier or more miserable than almost anything else.

It may be valuable to suggest taking a working hypothesis: 'Let's assume for the purpose of this course that there is a God, and see where that gets us.'

◾ The parenthood of God

One of our primary relationships for good or ill is that of the parent and the child. What do we look for in an ideal parent?

➔ Answers such as 'love', 'firmness' and 'stability' may be given. Some will require discussion, which should not be too prolonged – we are thinking about God, not parenting. In view of the poor experience which some within the group may have had of their own parents, gender differences should not be stressed, but rather the ideal looked for. The results should be written down on a sheet of paper on the floor.

God the Father has the characteristics of this ideal parent and these are shown to us through Jesus Christ – especially a love which sacrifices and is willing to suffer to help us.

What do we look for in the relationship of an ideal child to its parents?

→ Answers may include 'love', 'obedience' and 'helpfulness'. Show how all of these are dependent upon the trust of the child in the parent. Examine this idea of trust at some length, again writing the results on a sheet of paper.

If children are unsure of the love of a parent they will either try to 'earn' their love by doing well at school, by slaving around the house, by being unnaturally well-behaved, by buying expensive presents and so on; or they will rebel against the parents and go their own way. Neither is good: the first leads to a worried, over-conscientious person, and the second to someone who finds it difficult to trust others or make deep relationships.

God the Father has all that we look for in an ideal parent and much, much more.

We can behave like children who try to earn their parent's favour by giving 'presents' to our heavenly Father.

→ Ask for suggestions as to what these might be, and write them down on a series of 'presents', the outline of which has been drawn beforehand. Suggestions such as 'going to church' or 'being good' may be made.

Or we can rebel and try to forget about God. What form might this rebellion take?

→ Possibilities might be 'trying to forget about him', 'stopping going to church', 'behaving wrongly'.

Most of us do these at different times! This position of being separate from God is called 'sin' in the Bible. It describes the result of our attitude of being apart from God, either trying to deserve his love or turning our backs on him.

→ The story of the prodigal son found in Luke 15:11–24 can be told here in your own words. Do not go on to the story of the elder brother.

D Illustration

→ The following verbal picture can be used here, to draw
  together what has been said. It is on the video 'Session 1b:
  The Cottage'.

Think of a beautiful cottage that has become derelict. *(Get the
group to picture the cottage in their mind's eye.)* It was designed to be
perfect, a thing of beauty and an ideal home, but now it is broken
down and in need of thorough restoration. *(Help them to visualise
the overgrown garden, the broken windows, the rotting floorboards,
the holes in the roof, etc.)* Someone comes along who sees the
house, knows how it was intended to be and purchases it. He then
sets about restoring it to its former glory. Unlike most of us, he is
not an enthusiastic amateur but an experienced expert who knows
exactly what he is doing. He sets about his work of restoration in
precisely the right way for this particular cottage. Some jobs are
obvious and anyone looking at the cottage could see what he is
doing. Others are less obvious but nevertheless essential. He does
not give up until the work is complete.

Application: We have been 'bought with a price' and in Christ we
are being recreated into his likeness. God knows us and loves us as
individuals, he sees all our potential. Although sometimes his
work in our lives may seem drastic (like taking out *all* the floorboards!), he knows precisely what he is doing and we can trust
him not to do more in our lives at any one time than the structure
can take (the house is not going to collapse!). There will be times
as Christians when it is obvious what God is doing in our lives and
times when, though work is still going on, it will be less obvious.
He will not give up on us until his work is complete. Therefore, we
need not be frightened of change, because God knows what he is
doing. Neither need we be dismayed if at times he seems to be
more obviously at work in someone else than he is in us.

Christ came to show us that the Father's love does not have to be
earned, but is free – he loves us just as we are, and he longs to for-
give us and put right the break in relationships. More next week!

E Link-work

Link-work is an essential part of the course because it means that members can look carefully, with their Bibles, at the teaching that has been given.

→ Give out the link-work booklets at this point. If there are non-literate people in the group, audio tapes or some alternative to the link-work should be provided.

The introduction in the booklets gives some hints about daily prayer and Bible reading for those to whom this is something new.

→ If there is time, go through the main points of the link-work introduction.

The daily readings are to help people develop a pattern of daily prayer and Bible reading. The chunk readings (one per week) are from Mark and Acts, and cover the main events of Christ's life and the story of the early church. Although the chunk passages sound long, they are not excessive – Mark 1–8 is only eleven pages in the *Good News Bible*. The chunk readings are very important and should be seen as a priority. Point out that the question they should ask themselves during the chunk reading is printed in the link-work booklet (e.g. 'What sort of person was Jesus and what kind of things did he do?').

It will be useful for each member to get (or be given) a new notebook (A5) or exercise book to jot down answers to questions in the link-work as well as their own thoughts. They can also jot down questions they want to ask at the next session.

Link-work is not going to be inspected or marked. However, there will be an opportunity to ask questions or discuss difficulties at the beginning of most sessions. By the end of the course it is hoped that members will see the Bible as a well-loved and important book which they feel confident in using while being hungry for more of its teaching.

With some groups it will be necessary to check that members know how to use the index in their Bibles and can understand the notation for chapter and verse.

🅕 Prayer

Pray briefly, thanking God for his loving purposes for each person and for the change that is going to take place in each person's life during the course. Pray for the coming week. Say the Lord's Prayer (if it was not used at the beginning) and/or say the Grace together.

🅖 Refreshments

Encourage people to stay for refreshments.

1 Relationships

Notes before starting Session 1.

◆ If you have not yet read the Introduction, please do so before embarking on this session – it is very important.

◆ In the text, the basic teaching outline is given in normal serif type, while the ideas for the presentation are given in plain type (like this text) following an arrow ➔.

◆ It is assumed that the introductory meeting has been held before this session.

(Some parts of these notes on Session 1 apply to every session and are not repeated later.)

 ## Aims

◆ To introduce the members of the group to each other and to encourage openness and friendship between them.

◆ To show something of the character of God the Father, and the possibility of a relationship with him.

◆ To show the desirability of personal change and repentance and that this is linked to faith in God.

Leading the session

(It would be helpful to read the Introduction to Route A1 as some of this may also apply.)

The introductory meeting will have made clear the likelihood of personal change through taking the course. Course members should begin to look forward to the work of God in their lives. It should be shown to be exciting and desirable rather than threatening, though some may need help to see it in this light.

Obviously different groups will need different approaches to this first session, depending on their previous Christian background, their eagerness to progress and the number of questions they have.

This first session should see an apprehensive gaggle of individuals begin to turn into a group. Each will be nervous and rather defensive, and every effort should be made to help the group to relax and feel at home. Refreshments are useful on this occasion and a meal is a possibility if it is appropriate. There should certainly be something to encourage members to begin to chat with each other.

This and every session begins with the present experience of the course members. Thus this session begins with an examination of human relationships. Both Christians and non-Christians in the group will be able to identify with this and as many as feel able should be encouraged to contribute.

There is then a period of teaching on the personal character of God, emphasising in particular his love and his holiness – the latter seen as beauty and purity, rather than harsh judgement (it is the work of the Holy Spirit to convict of sin, not ours).

The understanding of the group members has to be considered, particularly in relation to the meaning of sin. For many people today, the idea of personal sin as an affront to the holiness of Almighty God is so foreign as to be meaningless, and the first session in particular should deal with matters which are readily understandable. On the other hand, the idea of relationships being formed and broken is part of the cultural norm of today, seen in a multitude of magazines and TV programmes.

The material may seem oversimple. However, experience has shown that these basic questions should not be skipped, even with groups made up of church members of some standing. In particular concentrate on those areas which are the experience of all in the room, to which all can make a contribution.

 Timing

Timing is given throughout the course in order to give an indication of the way in which the session could be spaced. However, it should never be kept to rigidly, and a good degree of flexibility should be used. This is particularly true in this first session where the leader is encouraging as many as possible to take part, is seeking to answer very basic questions, and where each member will come with very different questions to ask.

It is assumed throughout that each session lasts for 90 minutes.

0–10 mins	Prayer and A Introductions
10–25	B Change
25–45	C Relationships
45–70	D Broken relationships
70–90	Sections D–G of Route A Session 1b

Presentation

→ Members should be encouraged during this first session to raise points which have been troubling them, even if they are not relevant to the aim of this session – they may have been bottling them up for years. If a member raises a point which is strictly personal or intellectually beyond the range of the rest of the group, arrange to see them privately.

Begin with a brief prayer committing the evening to God.

A Introductions

The leaders should begin by introducing themselves to the group (even if this has been done at the introductory meeting – there was a great deal of information given at the meeting and names get forgotten).

There are a large number of 'introduction games' which can be played. If leaders know one which would be suitable, by all means use that, rather than the one suggested here. However, make sure that:

- people are not put in an embarrassing situation;
- it is not assumed that people can read aloud, or are confident enough to speak in a new situation (like the group);
- the game does not become an end in itself, or take too long;
- it is appropriate to the number of people you have and the size of the room you are meeting in;
- it does not assume any particular knowledge (e.g. of the Bible).

→ SUGGESTED 'INTRODUCTION GAME'

Give everyone a piece of A4 paper folded into four, and a pen/pencil. Ask each person to put:

- in the top left-hand corner – a picture or description of their favourite animal;
- in the top right-hand corner – their favourite colour;
- in the bottom left-hand corner – the name of someone they admire (dead or alive);
- in the bottom right-hand corner – the title of a book, film or TV programme which has meant a lot to them.

Ask them to discuss their choices with two people near them.

However, an introductory game is not essential. For example, you can simply gather people in triplets and ask them to say something about themselves to the other two.

Once the introductions have been made let the members voice their feelings. They may well arise naturally from the introductions but you can ask with a smile, 'What are you feeling?' The responses may well be those set out above in 'Leading the session'.

Acknowledge these views but do not spend too much time on them. It is a help to the group simply to know that others feel the same as themselves. It also gives them a chance to talk about their feelings.

→ If you wish, show the video 'Session 1a: Welcome to the course'.

B Change

God loves us and wants us to become in every way the people he created us to be. He wants us to enjoy 'life in all its fullness' (John 10:10). He does not want us to be simply 'good Christians' but mature men and women who are growing out of infantile and adolescent behaviour and relationships into wholeness of being.

During this course God is going to be at work in each person (see introductory meeting). His work will mean different things to different people (such as commitment to Christ, baptism in the Spirit, growing maturity and freedom in Christ) but for all it will mean change. We need not be afraid of change, as it is part of natural growth – no change is death.

→ Take time over this. Remember that the aim is to establish a positive expectation and desire for change. When explaining the sort of changes that may take place, terms like 'conversion' should probably not be used, but rather an explanation that for some the course may mean 'finding a new relationship with God' or 'discovering what it really means to be a Christian'. Concrete examples should be given throughout and the group encouraged to provide others.

→ You will find it useful to have read the Appendix at the back of this manual before this session in order to answer any questions which might arise at this point. However, this is not the time for a heavyweight theological discussion.

C Relationships

Ask the group: 'What brings us both the most happiness and the most misery?' Answer – relationships!

Good relationships lead to harmony, marriage, good homes and, on a wider level, to peace in the world and the well-being of all. The biblical word for this is 'shalom', which can be translated 'wholeness', 'integration', 'harmony at every level'.

→ An interesting way to develop this is to examine the network
   of relationships we have. On a piece of paper sketch an
   imaginary person, give him or her a name, and then link
   'Fred' or 'Elsie' with mother, father, those at work, children,
   neighbours, shopkeepers and so on. Then put in some of
   the cross-relationships, e.g. mother–father, boss–workmate.
   Emphasise that the closer the relationship is, the greater its
   potential for happiness or misery. (See page 11 for the best
   way to use this kind of visual aid in a group. You may find
   with a small number of people that it is best if you crawl
   about on the floor with a large sheet of paper – it is also a
   useful ice-breaker.)

If relationships with other people have such influence on our lives,
how much more important is our relationship with God? God is a
person – not a thing, an influence or a spiritual force – therefore he
can be loved, hated, worshipped or rejected.

→ There may be some who, although they have signed up for
   the course, still doubt the existence of God. If so, this needs
   to be thought through. It may be valuable to suggest taking
   a working hypothesis: 'Let's assume for the purpose of this
   course that there is a God, and see where that gets us.' Do
   not spend too long on this and beware of getting drawn into
   a purely intellectual discussion which will be of no real
   concern to the majority of the group.

ⒹBroken relationships

Discussion of broken relationships may well flow naturally from
Section C. Consider the effect of non-communication, barriers,
envy and pride on human relationships at both individual and
corporate levels. The example of an office, a hospital ward or a
school can be used to point out the effect of sin on society (national
or international examples may be too remote).

God created us to be in fellowship with himself and in harmony
with those around us. Our experience tells us that things are not as
they were meant to be. An inner restlessness tells us that we do not
experience true fellowship with God. St Augustine said, 'You have
made us for yourself and our hearts are restless till they find their

rest in you' or, as someone put it more recently, 'There is a God-shaped hole in every one of us.'

→ Encourage members to be honest about what they feel is their present relationship with God – many will be feeling the 'gap' and 'restlessness' in their own lives.

1 By wanting to go its own way, to be its own boss, the human race broke its relationship with God. This led to a barrier between God and us in the same way that any breakdown of relationships makes communication difficult or impossible. This barrier is what the Bible calls 'sin'. Sin is primarily an attitude of 'self' rather than the particular wrong actions to which that attitude leads. We try to lead lives independent of God with 'I' at the centre and the results are not impressive. *(Drive this home by thinking together of some of the unpleasant words which begin with 'self' – selfishness, self-indulgence, self-satisfied and so on.)*

→ It may take some time and discussion for the group to grasp the idea that sin is primarily attitude not actions – persist until you think it's beginning to sink in. While you are talking draw a simple picture with a felt-tip pen on a clipboard to illustrate this theme.

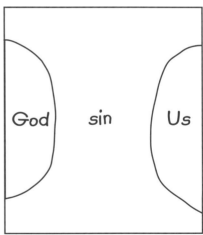

2 We cannot do anything to restore this relationship with God. From time to time most of us have tried – we start going to church, we 'turn over a new leaf', make resolutions and so on. This is so normal that for a lot of people being a Christian means going to church and being rather stuffily 'respectable'. But the fate of our efforts to reform ourselves is notoriously discouraging. We cannot find our way back to God and we cannot do anything about the barrier.

→ Discuss at length the ways in which we try to find God or 'inner peace'. Concentrate on this and how disappointing our efforts are. Use the visual aid and fill in the 'broken arrows' with the suggestions which are made.

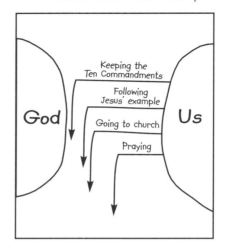

3 The impasse was broken by God taking the initiative and sending Jesus to break the barrier and restore communication. To find out how this happened, come next week!

→ It may be necessary, particularly if some of the group have been in contact with 'New Age' thinking, to emphasise that God is seeking for us. He loves us and takes the initiative. It is not a case of us seeking for a hidden God. Using a different coloured pen, complete the last visual aid so that the cross lies triumphantly over our failed efforts.

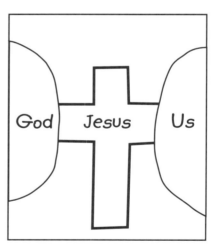

Section E and the rest of this session can be found in Sections D–G in Session 1b. Turn back to page 36.

2 Who is Jesus?

 Aims

◆ To help group members to come to an understanding of who Jesus is and what he has accomplished for us.

◆ To challenge them with the personal significance of the cross for each of us.

 Leading the session

The meeting begins by making the portrait of the person of Christ which course members have gained from the link-work. This verbal picture is the background to the video. It also has the effect of underlining the importance of the chunk reading.

'The Message of the Cross', on the video, despite its restrained handling of the Passion, always has a great impact. It is likely that the group will not be in the mood for discussion or comment afterwards, so go directly on to the response and the diagram of the four circles. The leaders will be doing most of the talking in this final period and members should not be forced to talk if they wish to be silent.

The video can be replaced by one from another source (e.g. the *Jesus* or *Jesus of Nazareth* videos), but these seldom have both the restraint and the stimulus to the imagination of the viewer shown by the Saints Alive! video. In particular, the challenge to commitment which immediately follows it is not given by other videos. Often this is better given by someone on screen, but whoever gives it, the challenge must not be omitted.

During this session the course members will be using their Bibles together for the first time. If there are people who are not used to handling the Bible, beware of excessive page-turning and wherever possible give page numbers as well as references.

 Timing

Because the initial work on the person of Christ can take a long time, it is important to ensure that ample time is left for the video. It is wise to set a time by which you intend to start Section D.

0–20 mins	Prayer, A Link-work, and the first part of B The person of Jesus
20–25	Remainder of B
25–40	C Who is he?
40–70	D The Passion (the video takes 18 mins)
70–87	E The importance of response (ending with Prayer)
87–90	G Link-work

Presentation

→ The video should have been set up before the group arrives and one of the leaders must know exactly which buttons to press: the effect should not be lessened by technical problems. The leaders should pray before and during the meeting, especially during the telling of the Passion, that people will respond to the love of God seen in Jesus. Try to set out chairs so that there is a minimum of rearrangement before and especially after the video.

Begin the session with prayer.

🅰 Link-work

Ask the group how they have got on and deal briefly with any questions or problems that have arisen. Explain that individual problems can be discussed at the end of one of the sessions or in the one-to-one meeting between Sessions 4 and 6.

🅱 The person of Jesus

The chunk reading of Mark 1–8 asked, 'What sort of person was Jesus and what kind of things did he do?' Ask the group what sort of words we might use to describe him, e.g. 'compassionate', 'strong', 'friendly' and so on.

→ Spend some time on this, encouraging every member of the group to make a contribution. Have ready some pieces of paper and felt tips, and write down the suggestions (you could do this yourself or get them to work in pairs), thus building up a verbal picture of Christ. Once again, the papers are best placed on the floor in the centre of the room. You may need to spend time considering some contrasting characteristics, e.g. anger and love. Keep the papers for possible use in Session 5.

We have built up a portrait of Jesus Christ – the complete human being. Notice that he is an utterly 'balanced' person, both sensitive and authoritative, caring and strong etc. Because he is fully human (notice if you have not already done so how he experienced hunger and thirst, sorrow and joy), everyone can identify with him and he knows how we feel. He has been through the whole range of human experience, so there is nothing we can go through that he cannot understand (see Hebrews 2:14–18; 4:15).

Notice, too, that Jesus began his public ministry when he was anointed with the Holy Spirit at his baptism. Get the group to flick through their Bibles and see that, apart from the birth stories and the visit to the temple in Luke, we know nothing of Jesus before this point. Why might this be?

→ This mention of the work of the Holy Spirit should not be laboured. It is, however, important at this early stage to link Christ's ministry with the coming of the Spirit at the River Jordan and show its significance.

◖ Who is he?

Read Mark 8:27–33 together. The time came when Jesus asked the disciples who others thought he was. Then he asked who they thought he was. There comes a point when all of us have to answer this question. Look at the answers that were given by the 'people': Jesus was not the kind of Messiah the Jews were expecting – not a military and political liberator nor a supernatural wonder-worker – he had rejected those models at the time of his temptations.

Peter was right: he was the Messiah, the Son of the living God (Matthew 16:16). But even Peter could not understand what that was to mean for Jesus. Jesus goes on to explain to them what it means for him to be the Messiah (Mark 8:31–38). He is the Suffering Servant, the Son of Man whose path to glory is the way of the cross.

➔ Before moving on to look at the events of the Passion, make sure that the group has really faced up to the question of who Jesus is. It may be helpful to look at some of his claims about himself, e.g. the 'I am' sayings (John 6:35; 8:12; 10:7, 11; 11:25; 14:6; 15:1). What sort of person could say such things? What does contemporary Christian experience say?

D The Passion

Move from Mark 8:31 to consider the climax of Jesus' ministry. Notice the proportion of the Gospels given to Passion Week.

➔ Let the group flick through their Bibles to verify this.

Explain that the events of that week are so important that it is good to put them into sequence and to see it whole. Even in church we often hear only of episodes. The video will be used for this.

➔ Show the video 'The Message of the Cross'. Many in the group, even those to whom the story is very familiar, will find the narrative very moving. (Pray for a spiritual rather than a simply emotional impact.) Do not expect an easy discussion afterwards. It may well be right to have a few minutes' silence followed by a prayer of thanksgiving.

E The importance of response

The end of the video reminds us that there are various responses we can make to the death of Christ. But we cannot do nothing – that in itself is rejection, for to ignore someone is to reject them. New Testament faith means to have Jesus right at the centre of our lives. Jesus died not only to free us from our sins, but to be Lord of all our lives. What this means can be illustrated by a simple visual aid.

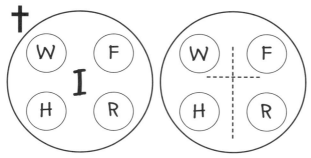

→ Draw a circle (on paper on the floor as usual) and explain that this circle represents our life. In the circle draw a series of smaller circles representing different aspects of our lives (F=family, W=work, R=relationships, H=hobbies). Put an 'I' in the centre and explain that this circle represents a life lived without God where 'I' decide what I will do (refer back to Session 1). The cross is outside the circle because Jesus has no place in this life. **The person who would not consider themselves a Christian.**

Draw a second circle identical to the first but with a faint dotted cross in it. This represents a life which used to be strongly Christ-centred but has allowed that faith to become a faint memory of long ago. **The nostalgic Christian.**

Draw another circle identical to the first but containing a small circle with a cross in it. Explain that this represents a life where the Christian faith and going to church is important, but is only really one interest among many and where the individual remains firmly in control. **The limited Christian.**

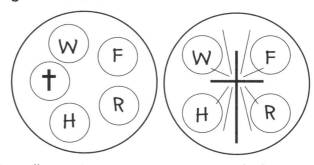

Draw a fourth circle where the central 'I' has been replaced by the cross. Jesus is allowed to be at the centre of our life. He is our Lord, and he influences every aspect of our being – our attitude to work, our political opinions, the way we spend our leisure, our relationships and so on. **The committed Christian.**

This is what Jesus died to achieve, for it is only when he is at the centre of our lives as Lord that we are truly ourselves, truly the people God created us to be.

→ This illustration has been found to be particularly helpful to those who would not consider themselves Christians and who have a vague 'spirituality' that is a significant part of their lives. It is also useful for those who have been going to church for years and for whom their faith, in so far as they have understood it, has been very important. The illustration does not ask people to deny their past but emphasises that we are all on a journey which takes us on from where we are towards understanding the meaning of fullness of life in Christ. With a group of mainly church people it is helpful to stress the need for continuing surrender and rededication of our lives to Christ, as we so easily push him from the centre.

F Prayer

Move from a consideration of our response to the love of God in Christ to a time of prayer. Either lead the group in prayers of adoration and thanksgiving or better still, if it seems right, encourage members to respond to God in a time of open prayer.

→ In practice, it has been found best not to lead in a prayer of commitment at this stage. Members will have an opportunity for a more considered response in Session 6. By that time they should have a fuller understanding of what they are doing and of the work of the Holy Spirit, and will not be pressurised by the emotional impact of the video or by group expectations. However, some may respond to God spontaneously in their hearts – in which case, praise him! It may be right to lead in a prayer in which each member of the group dedicates themselves to continue to seek God, to learn about him and to be prepared to change as he wishes.

G Link-work

Explain the link-work for the following week.

H Organisation

If this has not already been done, arrange dates for the remainder of the course.

3 'Risen, ascended, glorified'

Aims

◆ To give teaching on the resurrection and ascension.

◆ To help members to use the Bible for group study.

Leading the session

The session begins by exploring the human experience of death and contrasts it with the joy of the resurrection. Many may value the opportunity to talk freely about death for it is a largely forbidden subject, but there is a need to pass fairly quickly over this to the story of the resurrection.

Different groups will need different approaches to the fact of the resurrection. Some have few doubts and will want only a brief résumé, while others will wish to look into it thoroughly. A third group of people will have a personal belief in the resurrection but would like to have the facts set out so that they can feel confident in talking to others. The approach the leader uses will need to be very flexible and accepting. It is helpful to the doubters to point out that the early disciples were also uncertain about the resurrection and only came to a realisation of what had happened over a period of time.

For those groups which wish to examine the evidence for the resurrection in some detail, it is given on the video so that a fairly solid block of teaching can have the advantage of a fresh voice.

The Bible study on Luke 24 introduces a new method of teaching, and course members should be encouraged to follow the passage in their Bibles. Section C should flow into Section D with a break for the two main teaching points and the opportunity for testimony. Avoid a monologue: some groups may well be able to find out the answers for themselves, and this should be encouraged where possible. Ask frequently for comments. (If members are not using the same version of the Bible, give out photocopies of the passage.)

This session for the first time encourages course members to give a simple testimony to what God is already doing for them. It is often found that quite a number of the group have already got something to report, and they should be given every opportunity to share this. This can be a great encouragement to the others in the group, though stress that God works at different speeds in different people, and so there is no disgrace if nothing seems to have happened yet. This may also mean that the group is ready for open prayer at the end (or directly after Section D if it is felt that the time taken by administration will spoil the atmosphere).

> Good adult educationalists do not ask questions which most people in the group cannot answer. The teacher is put on a pedestal; the group members feel inadequate.

🕐 Timing

Because of the different approach that each group will need for Section C, timing will need to be adjusted – the time given is a suggestion.

0–12 mins	Prayer and A Link-work
12–25	B The experience of bereavement
25–45	C i) The resurrection (the video may be used)
45–65	C ii) Bible study on Luke 24:13–52
65–75	D Easter day: the evening and beyond
75–90	E Link-work, F Administration and G Prayer

There is a lot of material in this session and it is important to keep it flowing without seeming to rush. The administration is very important and can take some time. In some groups it can be best done over refreshments at the end where arrangements for the 'one-to-one meeting' can be made more informally. Leaders should pray about these meetings and decide beforehand which leaders should see each member.

 Presentation

Begin the evening with prayer.

🅐 Link-work

Deal briefly with any problems or questions that have arisen.

🅑 The experience of bereavement

→ This is not intended as bereavement counselling, but as a backcloth to the glory of the resurrection. However, personal grief may be brought to the surface which needs to be dealt with after the session.

Nearly all of us will have experienced the death of someone close to us, maybe quite recently. How did people react to us when they knew of our bereavement?

→ Members might speak of being ignored because others were embarrassed ('as though I were a pane of glass'), of a sentimental pity, of being told of the grief of others and so on.

How did we react?

→ Members will speak of the different stages of bereavement – numbness, anger, anxiety etc.

Why is there this difficulty in handling death? After all, it is natural enough. It is seldom that we talk sensibly about death, and even more rare that we talk of it with joy. Last week we looked at the very special death of Jesus – this week we shall go on with the story.

🅒 i) The resurrection

→ The telling of the story of the resurrection should be as vivid as possible, without straying from the biblical facts. Do not spend too long on this. Simply recount the story as best we know it, without getting the group to look it up in their Bibles.

Set the scene. The spring morning of the first Easter Day dawns upon a group of frightened, bewildered disciples. The grief-stricken women process to the tomb to anoint the body – and find it empty. The disciples doubt the women's story, but Peter and John run to the tomb and also find the body gone (but the graveclothes still in position). Mary Magdalene follows and arrives shortly afterwards. She is the first to see the risen Christ but at first does not recognise him through her tears. He speaks her name and she is overcome with joy. Go on to talk about the appearance to Peter (Luke 24:34); the still uncertain disciples going to Emmaus and the Christ who was known to them 'when he broke the bread'; the first appearance in the upper room that same Sunday evening.

1 Corinthians 15:3–8 shows us something of the number of appearances – those recounted in the Gospels are only a selection.

Where the group needs to have the main evidences for the resurrection set out, attention needs to be drawn to:

- the empty tomb;
- the graveclothes;
- the appearances after the resurrection (especially 1 Corinthians 15:3–7);
- the non-reaction of the authorities;
- the change in the disciples;
- the thrust of their preaching (see Acts 2:31–33; 10:40–41; 13:30);
- the continuing experience of the church.

→ This teaching can be given using the video.

◖ ii) Bible study on Luke 24:13–52

→ The rest of this section and much of the next is based on a leisurely reading through of Luke 24:13–52. It is not a detailed Bible study but rather an underlining of certain key points. The best approach is for all the group to follow it in their Bibles but for the leader to read it, encouraging participation from the course members and seeing what contributions they have to make. The following points can be made during the discussion. (A group which is mainly of church members can split into threes to read verses 13–32 in full and then discuss the passage. They can be given two questions: 'What is happening?' and 'What are the two disciples feeling?' The groups then report their findings.)

Introduce the passage by emphasising that the disciples were in no way programmed to believe that the resurrection would happen. Their first reaction was that it was 'nonsense (see Luke 24:11).

The Emmaus journey (Luke 24:13–32) This is a very modern story. Set the scene. The church, such as it is, is in Jerusalem. Cleopas and his companion (Mrs Cleopas?) are trudging away from the church, disheartened, disillusioned, confused, 'sad'. The stranger draws near (some group members may have become personally aware of the stranger in recent weeks – the new thoughts, an awareness of God's presence, a sense of being guided). He walks alongside them and draws out their feelings and experiences, without revealing who he is.

Luke 24:18–24 The whole of Cleopas's speech speaks of disappointed hopes, of being bereft of a leader, of perplexity. They are unwilling to put any weight on what the women have told them about the empty tomb and are leaving it all behind them.

Luke 24:26–27 The stranger shows how the crucifixion was not the terrible mistake they thought but is all part of the purposes of God and has been foretold in the Old Testament.

Luke 24:28–29 Jesus takes the initiative by coming to us: there comes a time when we have to make an appropriate response. They do so by inviting him to a meal. If they had not done so, he may have continued walking away. It was in the ordinariness of an everyday meal that he was recognised.

Luke 24:35 'Their eyes were opened and they recognised him...' The risen Christ has become personal for them. They run to tell others.

→ Pause at verse 34 and consider the significance of the resurrection for today. Take suggestions from the group wherever possible.

If Jesus lives, then what?

We can have eternal life as a present experience through faith (John 5:24). Eternal life is a new quality of life brought by Christ (contrast colour TV to black-and-white). Christian hope is not whistling in the dark – it is the certain faith that in Christ all will be well, and that even death is the doorway to being 'with Christ'.

Death is overcome. If we are Christians then we are joined with Christ and will ourselves experience resurrection from the dead. Death is no longer something to be feared: 'thanks be to God who gives us the victory through our Lord Jesus Christ'.

Encourage members to share their own recent experience of Christ. Have there been any changes in their life, new expectations, new hopes – even since the course began? Has the stranger begun to have a name?

➔ Normally two or three will already be able to speak of the difference Jesus is making in their lives. (People are often initially hesitant to speak. Do not worry if there is a considerable pause after you have invited contributions – only speak if you are certain no one has anything to offer.) Be prepared to spend time on this if the group is sharing freely.

D Easter Day: the evening and beyond

Read Luke 24:33–52.

Luke 24:39,43 Jesus emphasises that he is no ghost – he shows the reality of his body and eats the fish. The crucified leader is also the risen Lord who gives peace to his followers.

Luke 24:47 The tremendous news of the living Christ must be spread throughout the world.

➔ A visual aid can be sketched out on a round piece of paper on the floor with Jerusalem at the centre like a medieval map, with lines showing the gospel radiating out into the world. Put on it modern countries where group members know of Christian work.

Luke 24:49 But the disciples must first wait for the 'power from on high' which the Father has promised. We are not sent out alone into a hostile world – we too are given the Holy Spirit. More about this next week!

Luke 24:51 Christ's earthly life comes to a close, but soon his Spirit will be sent on his disciples (see John 16:7). The story of the ascension can be told graphically, mentioning the cloud, the parting words, the command to leave the place of ascension (Acts 1:6–11), but the important fact to convey is the glorification of Jesus and his present life 'to make intercession for us'.

Luke 24:52 They are joyful and prayerfully expectant.

→ Do not anticipate the next session by telling the story of Pentecost, but try to get the group to have the same sense of rather mystified expectancy that the disciples had.

◨ Link-work

Explain the link-work for the coming week.

◧ Administration

This could be done over refreshments – see 'Timing' above.

Arrange to meet all the members of the group individually at some point between Sessions 4 and 6. Explain that this is not an inquisition but an opportunity for the leaders to get to know the course members better, and for course members to be able to ask questions and talk about things they might not want to discuss in the group.

→ Allow about one-and-a-half hours for each one-to-one meeting. It is best if they take place in the homes of the members as they are then more relaxed (unless, of course, home circumstances would make it difficult to see the person on their own).

◪ Prayer

Pray either here or at the end of Section D. Encourage members to join in a time of open prayer and praise as they consider what it means that Jesus is the risen Lord.

4 Who is this Holy Spirit?

Aim

◆ To help people to understand the work of the Holy Spirit (praying that they may become thirsty to know his power in their own lives).

Leading the session

In Sessions 4 and 5 the work of the Holy Spirit is explored. It is important that the work of the Spirit is seen as a normal part of the Christian life and everything should be done to make it matter-of-fact. There may be a danger in using examples which are too far from the experience of course members. This is particularly true when the gift of tongues is discussed, and it may be useful to bring forward the idea of the tool bag from Session 5 to emphasise the unremarkable nature of the gift (do not, however, anticipate the teaching on gifts in Session 5). On the other hand, do not miss out the teaching on tongues which comes naturally in the discussion of Pentecost. It is important to state clearly that tongues are not essential to baptism in the Spirit.

Whether or not to use the phrase 'baptism in the Spirit' or 'anointing with the Spirit' should be decided by the leaders – it may be a difficulty for some group members who are theologically trained. The Appendix can be used to explain to them privately where it fits into the whole pattern of Christian initiation. You may photocopy the Appendix for such a person, if you wish to.

By this stage in the course the members should be talking freely, and their own experience should be called for and used wherever possible. Be prepared to bring fears to the surface when they are hinted at.

The one-to-one meetings are generally looked forward to by course members, but some may be apprehensive, so do not make it seem a frightening 'interview' but a normal part of the course.

 **Timing**

0–10 mins	Prayer and A Link-work
10–18	B Recap and introduction
18–40	C The events of Pentecost
40–70	D The Spirit today
70–85	E Personal experience (the video may be used)
85–90	F Link-work and G Prayer

 **Presentation**

Begin the evening with prayer.

A Link-work

Deal with any problems that have arisen.

B Recap and introduction

In Acts 1:1–5 Luke reminds Theophilus of what was said at the end of his Gospel (see Session 3).

Acts 1:3–5 Although for the purpose of this course it is convenient to see the cross, the resurrection and Pentecost as separate, they are in fact one 'event' in the great purposes of God for his church and the world.

Acts 1:5 We are reminded of John's baptism and the beginning of the ministry of Jesus (see Session 2). John had prophesied that Jesus would be the one who 'baptises with the Holy Spirit'. It was this 'promise of the Father' that the disciples were to wait for.

C The events of Pentecost

→ Although the group will have read Acts 1 and 2 in their link-work, it is useful to recap, drawing out the following points to ensure that they have grasped the main thoughts. The narrative can be told in a connected way by one of the leaders, but preferably elicited by question and answer from the group. The question might be asked, 'What do you see as the most important points of these two chapters?' The order in which the points emerge is not important. (The references are given for the benefit of the leaders – it is not necessary to draw the attention of the group to each one.)

- Before Jesus ascended he promised that the Holy Spirit, who would be given to the disciples, would give them power to enable them to tell others about him (1:8).
- They met together for prayer while they waited for the gift of the Holy Spirit (1:14).
- When the Holy Spirit came at Pentecost (the Jewish harvest festival), something definite happened which they described in terms of wind and fire (2:1–3). Note the use of the word 'like': we often have to use picture language when describing our experiences of the Lord.
- All the disciples were filled with the Holy Spirit and spoke in tongues (2:4). These were other languages which could be understood by foreigners in the crowd.
- The crowd gathered and heard about the great works of God in a way that they could understand (2:11).
- Division was caused among the crowd (2:12).
- Peter, a radically changed man, stood up in a potentially hostile situation to explain what was happening (2:14–39).
- Peter said that the gift of the Holy Spirit is for everyone, not just special people (2:17).
- People in the crowd were deeply moved. They repented and acknowledged Jesus as Lord and were filled with the Spirit (2:37–39, 41).
- A new community was founded where much love was seen in action and the power of God worked through them. They were eager to worship and learn more of God (2:43–47).

D The Spirit today

→ In order that the very important teaching of this section
strikes home, prepare beforehand sheets of paper with the
words printed in bold below, and produce them at the
appropriate points.

The Holy Spirit was not just given to the first disciples – Jesus
promised to give the Holy Spirit to all who believe in him. He still
gives the Holy Spirit to people today.

→ It is important that there should be many references to
present-day personal experience. At this point, one of the
leaders should give their testimony about the time when they
were baptised in the Holy Spirit. Possibly some of the group
can add their experience. Any testimonies should be given
straightforwardly and not at too great length. The
'ordinariness' of the experience should be emphasised
rather than its 'extraordinariness' – the important point is the
difference it made to life. Say nothing that suggests there is
a certain blueprint which must be copied, and stress that for
some it is very quiet, while for others it is much more obvious. The thing that matters is not what we feel but the results
of the infilling of the Spirit in serving others and being close
to God.

The testimony on the video can be used here or at Section E.

There are some important things we need to know about this gift
of the Holy Spirit.

→ Some of these points may have been made during the
testimony. However, it is a good idea to highlight them
briefly, maybe referring back to what has just been said.

● **Something definite takes place.** God the Holy Spirit will come
– for the first disciples it meant an overwhelming experience
which they described in terms of wind and fire. The group
members should not expect the same experience as the person
next to them. God deals with each of us differently, as he knows
what is best for each one of us.

- **The character of Jesus begins to be formed in us through his Spirit.** Paul calls this the fruit of the Spirit (Galatians 5:22) – love, joy, peace, patience, kindness, goodness, faithfulness, humility and self-control. More teaching will be given on this next week.

- Because love is one of the fruits of the Spirit **we will find ourselves drawn towards other Christians**. This is Christian fellowship. It means being involved with others, sharing our lives with them, respecting and helping one another (see Acts 2:44–47). Some may already be feeling this desire to meet with others.

- **We are given the Holy Spirit in order that we may serve other people**: it is not primarily for ourselves. After his baptism Jesus began to minister to people; after Pentecost the disciples went out to serve. Baptism in the Spirit is not a nice 'spiritual experience' to be sought for its own sake. The gift of the Spirit is given so that God can work through us to help other people.

➔ The fact that we are baptised in the Spirit not primarily for ourselves but in order to serve God better in the world is of the greatest importance and should be stressed here and at every other possible occasion.

- When the Holy Spirit is working freely in our lives, **we will find it easier to speak about Jesus**, because his work is to glorify Jesus (John 16:14). Peter, who had been so cowardly, was prepared to stand in front of a hostile crowd after he had been filled with the Spirit.

- People speak in tongues or are given other gifts of the Spirit when they ask to be filled with the Spirit. Tongues were exercised publicly at Pentecost, but often they are given as a private prayer language for building up our spiritual life (1 Corinthians 14:4).

➔ For some the idea of tongues may be new or threatening, while for others it is a normal part of church life. Newcomers usually find it presents no difficulty. Do not overemphasise it, but if there are questions reassure them:

  ~ Praying in tongues is as much under our control as if we were praying in English.

~ We don't understand it but it does us good!

~ We do not have to be in an emotionally or spiritually exalted state of mind in order to speak in tongues.

~ Further teaching on the gifts of the Spirit will be given in the next session.

● Above all, **we will find ourselves wanting to worship God** because by the Spirit's power we cry out to God 'Abba, Father' (Romans 8:15). Particularly we will be drawn to worship God with other Christians, as happened after Pentecost (Acts 2:46).

E Personal experience

Can any members of the group who have been baptised in the Spirit illustrate any of the above points from their experience?

→ The testimony on the video can be used at this point. Lead into a general discussion, where you encourage members to bring up any questions, doubts or comments.

F Link-work and administration

Explain the link-work and check that the arrangements made last week for the one-to-one meetings are still all right. Encourage group members to think of, and jot down, any questions they want to ask or any personal matter which it is important to talk about.

G Prayer

End with a time of relaxed prayer. Be open to the Holy Spirit who may underline the teaching by giving gifts of prophecy or tongues and interpretation.

One-to-one meeting

→ The purpose of this time with each member is to ensure that each individual is seen as of equal worth. In group meetings it is easy to give more attention to those who talk most or who present obvious problems. The time alone with each member often presents a very different picture than has been seen before in the group.

This is an admirable opportunity to help each one to express their feelings, fears and expectations. Furthermore, it is important for course leaders to be aware of the spiritual position of each member before Session 6.

When you first meet, do everything possible to put the course member at ease. They may well feel rather nervous. A period of general conversation over a cup of tea will help them to relax. You can then talk about the course and the impact it is having on them. Try to memorise the following points and cover them in the course of your discussion – they do not have to come up in any particular order (the sight of any piece of paper will immediately make you seem like an interviewer and this should be avoided).

Assure the course member of complete confidentiality between you.

- Has their experience of the course been stimulating, confusing (explain that confusion is often the starting point of a fresh idea), difficult...?
- Has the fellowship they have encountered meant anything new to them? (Usually this is one of the most positive points in the course so far.)
- How have they got on with the link-work? Has it been too much for them? (It is often found that course members do the daily portions in one or two sessions during the week rather than as a daily discipline. This should not be frowned on: the important thing is that they are reading their Bible.)
- Have they any questions arising from the course – intellectual or moral? Has the person of Jesus Christ come alive? Have they any questions about baptism in the Spirit?

- Has the experience of God in their own lives in prayer and Bible reading led to growth in spiritual understanding and perception? Can they see a crystallising of their previous knowledge of spirituality?

- Do they really know what becoming a Christian will mean to them in their personal lives and the cost involved? (Often points about the ethical issues raised by their work or home life are brought out here. Avoid glib answers and do not be afraid to say 'I don't know': often people just need to talk a matter over with someone who can listen sympathetically.)

- Is anything particularly on their conscience? It is essential that there should be a deep understanding of repentance and a thorough self-examination before ministry. The offer of a more formal act of penitence may be appropriate.

- Has there been any involvement with the occult? (On the one hand avoid any inquisition which sets the person worrying about trifles, but on the other, explore this area sensitively. Nearly always plain repentance and trust in Christ is the only healing required, but deliverance may be indicated. Never undertake deliverance without consulting and working with someone else. An opportunity to discuss the occult more fully is given in Session 5D.)

- Are they willing to commit themselves to Christ and his people, remembering that none of us is ever wholly worthy?

End with a brief prayer for the person and their home situation, any people who have been mentioned, other course members and the time of ministry.

5 Harvest time – fruit and gifts

 ## Aims

◆ To teach about the fruit and gifts of the Spirit.
◆ To prepare members of the group to give themselves to Christ and be filled with the Holy Spirit.

 ## Leading the session

There is a danger that the fruit of the Spirit may be seen as less interesting than the gifts, particularly as some of the gifts like prophecy etc were mentioned in the last session. Therefore spend time on Section B and do not allow Sections D and E to be cut short by excessive time spent on Section C.

The video gives teaching on the gifts of the Spirit and some illustrations of how they have been used in ordinary situations. John Finney's teaching gives a concise overview and may save time in what is a very full session.

The group should be beginning to look forward to Session 6 – some with an understandable sense of apprehension. Encourage a calm expectancy and openness to what God has to give.

Timing

0–10 mins	Prayer and A Link-work
10–30	B The fruit of the Spirit
30–50	C The gifts of the Spirit (the video may be used)
50–65	D i) Repentance
65–80	D ii) Trust
80–90	E Next week, F Link-work and G Prayer

 Presentation

Begin the evening with prayer, or maybe postpone prayer for
Section B.

A Link-work

Deal with any problems that have arisen, and ascertain, if possible,
the amount of spiritual nourishment which is being received from
the link-work by group members.

→ This gives an opportunity to evaluate the link-work alongside
what you are learning from the one-to-one meetings. It
can lead on without a break to Section B and the time for
sharing and prayer.

B The fruit of the Spirit

Last week we began to think about the changes brought about in
our lives by the Holy Spirit. Has anything happened this week
which is good and an indication that he is already at work in the
members' lives bringing change?

→ Allow a brief time for sharing. It might be helpful to ask the
group to think back to the beginning of the course and
remember any changes that have happened since then.
Often the group will be very encouraged when they discover
what is already happening in their lives, and such a time of
sharing can lead naturally into a time of thanksgiving with
individuals contributing short prayers.

Read Galatians 5:19–26.

→ Put the different 'fruit' on pieces of paper and throw them
onto the floor as you slowly read verses 22 and 23.

The phrase translated in the Good News Bible as 'the Spirit
produces' (v. 22) is translated elsewhere as 'the fruit of the Spirit'
or 'the harvest of the Spirit'. Look at the contrast between 'what
human nature does' and 'what the Spirit produces'. God wants us
to become like his Son Jesus (Romans 8:29). The fruit of the Spirit
is the character of Jesus himself being produced over a lifetime
within his people. This does not make us clones of Jesus but

strengthens and develops the personality we have. (Illustrate by some strong-minded Christian you know from history or personal acquaintance.)

→ Produce the bits of paper with the verbal picture of Jesus which were created during Session 2 and put them alongside the 'fruit'. Discuss how they dovetail.

Two things to note about the fruit of the Spirit:

● Fruit is a natural product of a healthy tree – effort is not required on the part of the tree in order to produce fruit. Our characters will become more like the character of Jesus by 'remaining in him', not by strenuous self-improvement techniques (see John 15:4–5). This is particularly important if some in the group have been involved in various self-fulfilment programmes and been disappointed by the results.

● Fruit is something more easily seen by an onlooker: often others are far more aware of changes in us than we are ourselves.

→ Members can be asked if others have commented on the changes which are taking place in their lives, but not in such a way as to discourage those who are still working things out.

◉ The gifts of the Spirit

Last week we thought particularly about the gifts of prophecy and tongues because those were most evident on the day of Pentecost, and we noticed that other signs and wonders were an ordinary part of the church's life.

→ Ask the group briefly what signs and wonders they have read about as they have done their chunk reading of Acts.

However, the gifts of the Spirit are not necessarily dramatic – they are simply the tool kit which God has given us to use as we go about his business in the world.

→ The following teaching about the tool box and the nine gifts of the Spirit in 1 Corinthians 12 is given on the video, if you wish to use it.

Before the session, make a simple visual aid with outlines of
nine common tools (chisel, hammer, drill, ruler and so on)
and the nine gifts of the Spirit listed in 1 Corinthians
12:4–11. If you wish, you can try to fit each gift with what
you consider to be an appropriate tool, but do not be over-
ingenious: it is best to be simple. Alternatively write each gift
on a tag and tie them to nine different tools and bring them
in a tool box. Now bring out your handiwork!

In 1 Corinthians 12:4–11 we have a list of these gifts. (The list is
not exhaustive: see also Romans 12 and Ephesians 4.) Read the
passage and before looking at each gift in turn, note:

- there are different kinds of gifts, different ways of serving and
  different abilities to perform service – that is, different people
  need different tools for different jobs;

- they all come from the same source (v. 4);

- everyone can perform their 'particular service' for the good of
  all (vv. 6,7); tools are meant to be used to do something
  constructive which will help others.

➔ Run through the nine gifts of the Spirit, giving a brief
  explanation of each and how it can be used in practice. Or
  use the teaching given in the video.

  Give examples of using the gifts of the Spirit from your own
  experience or from the testimonies on the video. They should
  be as down-to-earth as possible.

  There will probably be some people in the group who can
  recall times when they have been able to help someone by
  saying 'just the right thing', although they were unaware
  of it at the time, or of being on the receiving end of such
  help. Point out that these may be examples of the gifts of
  knowledge and wisdom.

  If there are others in the group who have been baptised in
  the Spirit, encourage them to share their experiences of the
  gifts. There is sometimes a tendency for people to think that
  only leaders are given such things.

☑ Preparing to receive

God does not want us simply to talk about new life in Jesus and the gift of his Spirit. He wants us to know these things for ourselves. In Acts 2:37 the crowd said to Peter, 'What shall we do?' and Peter replied, 'Each one of you must turn away from your sins and be baptised ... for God's promise was made to ... all whom [he] calls to himself.' Peter was talking about repentance and trust (faith). We shall look at each in turn.

Repentance

Repentance is a 'change of direction':

- a turning away from things which spoil our relationship with God;
- a turning towards God.

→ The first action is to recognise self-centredness. This can be demonstrated with a simple visual aid drawn at the time. The double action of repentance can be shown by a circle representing our life, with a capital 'i' representing self in the centre. The second action of repentance can be illustrated by putting a bar across the 'I' so that the cross can be shown to be at the centre of our lives.

Basically what we are turning away from is our self-centredness which puts 'I' at the centre of our lives (recall Sessions 1 and 2). However, the New Testament also talks about turning away from specific sin. In Galatians 5:19–21, which we have already read, we have one such list. Notice the scope of the list – although it is not comprehensive, it includes everything from witchcraft to jealousy. We need to examine ourselves before God and see if there is some particular sinful attitude or action which has a hold on our life and needs to be renounced. Repentance is a decision not a feeling.

This is particularly true of anything to do with the occult, and members of the group should be asked to mention in their one-to-one meeting any personal involvement they may have had with black magic, crystals, ouija boards, horoscopes, tarot cards, mediums, spiritualist healing and so on.

→ It may well be right to ask group members to mention in the one-to-one meeting any sin which has an unshakeable grip upon them. The confession of this before a minister and the pronouncement of God's forgiveness will bring release.

Trust

Peter asked in Acts 2:37 that the people should not only repent but be baptised as a sign of their trust in Christ as Lord and Saviour. Trust, or faith, is a reliance on God, and on what he has promised. Like repentance, it is a decision we take:

I repent of my sins... I renounce evil... I turn to Christ

➔ (Anglican note: it was agreed by General Synod that these promises should stand alongside those given in *Common Worship*.) A link with the liturgical promises of baptism or some other commitment prayer such as that used by Methodists at the New Year is helpful in showing that we are following the usual teaching of our denomination. It would be unwise at this point to embark on a full explanation of baptism! Here it is seen simply as a profession of faith – as it was on the day of Pentecost. It is useful however to mention the promises of baptism if they may be used in the time of ministry in Session 6.

Peter said that if the people repented and believed then:

● **their sins would be forgiven;**
● **they would receive God's gift, the Holy Spirit.**

The people believed what he had said and repented and trusted in God. Our Christian lives do not depend on our feelings at any particular time, but upon the character and promises of God. Of the 3,000 who were baptised at Pentecost, some would have been ecstatic, some would just have felt it was the right thing to do, while others would have felt nothing at all.

E Next week

At next week's session there will be an opportunity to respond to what has been heard over the past few weeks. The pattern of the session will not be the same as usual so it will be helpful if the course members know in advance what is going to happen.

After a short time of teaching, everyone who wishes can dedicate their lives to God through Jesus Christ and receive the laying on of hands for the baptism in the Holy Spirit. Those who are already Christians and who know the fullness of the Spirit in their lives will also have the opportunity to rededicate their lives and pray for their ministry within the body of Christ.

→ Explain in broad outline the mechanics of what you propose to do at the next session:

- Where they will go to receive ministry.
- Ministry will involve prayer and the laying on of hands with one of the leaders.
- There is no compulsion for anyone to receive ministry who feels they are not ready for it.

For the domestic convenience of the members, tell them that they will probably not all be leaving at the same time and that some may be later home than usual.

⬛ Link-work and administration

Check that each person knows when and where their one-to-one meeting will take place. Run through the link-work.

⬛ Prayer

Praise God for his love and pray specifically that at the next session everyone in the group will take the step towards God that he wants of them. Aim to build up faith and expectancy.

6 Time for ministry

 ## Aim

◆ To continue teaching on the work of the Holy Spirit and to offer the opportunity for each member to respond and receive the appropriate ministry.

 ## Leading the session

In some ways this is the key session of the course and you will need to pray for great sensitivity in leading it. Pray that each member will take the step or steps towards God which are right for them. At some point during the session an opportunity for open response must be given.

At the beginning the leaders prayed that the right people would come onto the course. God did not bring them along for nothing, so to avoid offering ministry is to sell them short and is a pastoral failure. In practice it has been found that the great majority of Saints Alive! group members wish to receive ministry.

Faith is required by the leaders, and very few approach Session 6 without some qualms – indeed it is probably an indication of poor leadership if there is not a feeling of excited apprehension. The reason for our unease is that we are saying to God, 'Over to you,' and we are therefore not in control.

With a very large group there is sometimes a wish to bring in other people you trust to help with the ministry. It is best if this can be avoided since these people have not shared in the life of the group nor taken part in the one-to-one meetings. Members may resent what can be seen as the intrusion of 'strangers' at a time which is very personal and precious. However, if there are Christians in the group who have already been baptised in the Spirit, they may well be invited to join in the ministry after they themselves have been ministered to.

Before the session the leaders should have a meeting with plenty of time available to pray for each member of the group by name. (The one-to-one meetings of the previous weeks will have indicated the direction that prayer should take.) The leaders should each rededicate themselves to God and to caring for the course members. They should lay hands on each other with the prayer that they should be open to the promptings of the Spirit during the session. It has been found to be helpful if this time of prayer can be in the place where the ministry will occur.

The teaching in this session is short and straightforward and the essential element in the session is the ministry to course members – what leaders do is more important than what they say.

While there is part of the ministry which can never be planned for, great care should be taken with the practical arrangements. The 'mechanics' of the time of ministry are important and should be carefully thought through beforehand. The requirements are:

- Reasonable privacy – so that the individual can talk unheard by the other members of the group. This can be arranged by being some distance from the others or by some covering noise such as soft singing or taped music.
- Suitable conditions for receiving the laying on of hands – not easy if folk are squashed together on a sofa!
- A situation where there is not undue pressure on an individual to receive ministry if they do not feel that they are ready for it. There is bound to be some unavoidable pressure because the course has been leading up to this session, but this should not be increased by 'no escape' surroundings.
- The freedom to express emotion if it genuinely needs an outlet – paper tissues should be available.
- Surroundings of some peace and beauty are helpful as the place where they receive ministry will become for some of the course members a 'holy ground'.

It is possible for ministry to take place in the room where the sessions usually happen, but privacy is usually difficult and the group pressure to conform can be formidable. It has been found to be best if members who wish to receive ministry move physically from one place to another – the movement itself becomes a sign of commitment. In practice many have found it helpful to have the ministry in church. If so the first part of the session can be in the church or a room nearby. After the teaching in Sections A–D it can be explained where the leaders are going, and that those who wish to receive ministry can follow when they're ready. Those who do not so wish are bade 'goodbye' and 'see you next week'. If the time of ministry is to take place in a church, the people can sit in the body of the church and then come to the communion rail or similar point for ministry. The leader can initially kneel on the opposite side of the communion rail in order to be able to talk at the same level and then stand for the laying on of hands: he or she then kneels again to encourage the person being ministered to to speak words of praise (or tongues).

There will inevitably be a certain amount of anxiety around. Leaders will need to explain in some detail, and more than once, exactly what they are expecting people to do – lack of certainty about this will make nerves jangle unnecessarily.

Timing

The timing of this session is both difficult and important. It has been found that excessively long sessions sometimes occur when leaders forget that this is not a counselling session but an opportunity to minister to each individual in the power of the Spirit through the laying on of hands with prayer. Aim at half an hour for the opening teaching and not more than one-and-a-half hours for the time of ministry.

Leaders should remember that time seems to go very fast when you are ministering to people – while it may seem much slower to those who are waiting to receive ministry. Leaders should not be so absorbed in ministry that they forget the needs of those who are still waiting.

Ministry to a big group can take some time, for there must be no sense of rush. In practice it has been found that ministry to each person takes between four and ten minutes.

It is good for the leaders to minister together (assuming there are two), with one leading the ministry and the other standing back to pray and to wait upon the Lord for specific words of wisdom for the person concerned. However, if there are a large number, or one individual appears to need a more prolonged time of ministry, it is wise for them to divide and minister singly.

 Presentation

A Link-work

Since every individual has had a chance to see one of the leaders during the previous two weeks, and time is short, leave any questions until next week. However, invite questions which have to do with the ministry and the baptism of the Spirit so as to unearth any private fears which may still be lurking.

B Luke 11:1–13

This Bible passage and the following give 'instructions' on receiving the Holy Spirit, and these elements should be highlighted and may be alluded to in the time of ministry. Go through this passage making the following points:

● The disciples had a desire for a deeper experience of God (v. 1).

● There is need for persistence and seriousness of purpose in asking for the Spirit: it is not a spiritual ego trip (v. 8; it may be necessary to point out that the parable is not about God's reluctance).

● The promise is sure: those who ask will receive (vv. 9–10). The Spirit is received by faith not by feelings.

● God never gives us dangerous or stupid gifts (vv. 11–12). Therefore we should have no fear of any gift from our heavenly Father (see Matthew 7:11, 'good gifts').

● We must ask for the Spirit to be given to us (v. 13). Baptism in the Spirit rarely happens 'spontaneously'.

ⒼJohn 7:37–39

Read through the passage and make the following points:

1 Verse 37 speaks of three stages: thirsting, coming, drinking (illustrate with an imaginary glass of water).

● Verse 38 shows that streams go out from the Spirit-filled person into the world: he or she should be an oasis in the desert to serve others.

Ⓓ Prayer

A time of prayer led by the leaders should finish this first part of the session and lead into the time of ministry. (If you are moving to a different place, pray both after the first part and in the new surroundings.) The prayers should be simple prayers of thanksgiving and expectancy which will help people to step out in trust.

Ⓔ The time of ministry

→ Throughout this session try to be relaxed and let humour break through. Remember that when you are ministering your own feelings of inadequacy and self-consciousness are unimportant – it is God whom we are expecting to see in action.

Explain to those who wish to be ministered to exactly what you are expecting them to do, e.g.:

● Where they are to receive ministry.

● Whether they should stand, sit or kneel.

● What they should do while they are waiting (pray).

● What they should do afterwards (normally pray quietly for a while, practising any gift of tongues which God has given, and then go home; some however will want to share in the ministry by staying to pray for their fellow course members).

→ While it is impossible to set out a blueprint of how to minister to each person, the following outline has been found to be useful. It is based on the three promises made at baptism mentioned in Session 5. It has been found that the semi-formal feel of the words is helpful and enables those being ministered to to start to speak. They should always be followed by an opportunity for the person to express the prayer of commitment in their own words.

First ask the person who has come for ministry if they wish to repent of the past and begin afresh. If so, they will find it helpful to say aloud after you: *'I repent of my sins.'*

Ask them if they need to pray to get rid of any wrong things in the past which still have an influence. This is particularly important if they have had any occult involvement. *'I renounce evil.'*

Then ask them if they are a Christian or wish to become one. If so, they can then say to you: *'I turn to Christ.'*

They will find it a great help if they can then sum this up in an audible prayer to God in their own words. If they find this difficult they can repeat a prayer of commitment after you.

→ Much of this may have been covered at the one-to-one meeting and can be omitted, but audible prayer should always be included before ministry proceeds.

When going on to pray for baptism in the Spirit, first ask if they want to be filled with the Holy Spirit. If they agree, then lay hands firmly, but not heavily, on their head and ask Jesus to fill their lives completely with his Spirit. Kneel or sit down beside them and encourage them to praise God out loud. Then, as release comes through audible prayer, encourage them to speak in tongues. You may need to spend some time with them encouraging them to relax and overcome their inhibitions (they may well never have spoken audibly in prayer with another person present before). It can be helpful, at times, to invite them to copy your tongue, and as they yield their voice to God in obedience they will find they are no longer copying your words, but praying their own. Alternatively, repeating words like 'Abba', 'Alleluia', and 'Hosanna' can help to unlock their tongue.

→ The more relaxed we are, the easier it will be for the person being prayed for. Laughter is a great gift of God at this point. Take your time as you pray for people and do not move from one part of the ministry to the next until you are sure that they are ready.

Do not be alarmed if there are physical manifestations as the Holy Spirit releases pent-up emotions – crying, laughing, shaking and even 'resting in the Spirit' are all quite common. Do not be worried by this or disappointed if nothing seems to be happening. God is doing his work in them, and it is not for us to dictate how we would like it to happen. (It may be important to reassure other members of the group if somebody responds to prayer in a particularly dramatic fashion!)

This is not a counselling session for the discussion of problems. The important thing is to minister to each individual in the power of the Spirit through the laying on of hands with prayer.

If there are any Christians in the group who have already been baptised in the Spirit, they could be encouraged to rededicate their lives to Christ and to pray for their ministry in the life of the church. They too should receive the laying on of hands with prayer.

If husbands and wives are present together it may be right to minister to them together. It is a great joy if they can enter together into the experience of the Holy Spirit.

7 Growing up

Aim

◆ To help people understand what has happened to them and to encourage further growth in Christ.

Leading the session

The session does not begin with prayer and link-work as usual. People often start to share what has happened to them in Session 6 and in the past week as soon as they meet. If this happens it is more natural not to break into this with a formal start but to take the stories which are being told and use them as pegs on which to hang the appropriate teaching.

Just as Peter explained what had been happening to the crowd at Pentecost, so we need to help people to interpret their experience. The session needs careful handling because of the different experiences of each member. Some may feel magnificent, some may have had a feeling of anticlimax, some may be quietly rejoicing. It is important that the enthusiasm of the joyful is not allowed to swamp the disappointed. A few may not have received ministry at all, and they can be invited to receive ministry at this session or later.

Pick up the experience of course members to link with the teaching. Some will have had a very emotional time and will need to have their experience based on the facts of the gospel. Others will have encountered opposition and will need to hear teaching on this. Those who are seeing their commitment to God in terms only of a personal blessing need to have the priority of the service of others stressed – indeed this becomes one of the main themes of the remainder of the course as we pass from the individual and God to think of the individual in the church and the world.

The teaching is likely to be best if it is not necessarily given in the order set out here, but in direct response to the experiences which members recount.

The session ends with a rapid look at some of the ways God uses to help us to grow: this is not intended to be a complete course on the Bible, the sacraments and Christian witness. That should come after the course is finished. Rather it is a summary and an appetite-whetter for teaching which needs to come later.

Have ready appropriate Bible reading notes for course members to look at.

Timing

Note that the length of the notes in this manual is no guide to the time which should be taken in the meeting. In particular Section D is intended as a summary, not an exhaustive exposition of the subjects mentioned.

0–35 mins	A Discussion and B Facts and feelings
35–55	C Afterwards
55–80	D Continued growth (The video may be used)
80–90	E Prayer

Presentation

A Discussion

→ During the discussion, watch for opportunities to bring in some of the teaching contained in the rest of this session.

Invite members to share what God has been doing in their lives over the past week, including the difficulties and disappointments they may have had.

→ Often joy will be the predominant note of this session but watch for any who are not sharing it, and offer further ministry to them afterwards if appropriate.

If people can articulate the work of Christ in their lives within the group, it will be easier for them to speak of him outside. Therefore encourage all to take part in this time of sharing.

N.B. This is an important part of the session, so do not be too ready to draw the discussion to a close.

B Facts and feelings

We are meant to be sure that we are Christians; 1 John was written specifically to assure us of that. Read 1 John 5:13.

Feelings may come and go, but our faith is founded on fact:
● the fact of Christ's death and resurrection;
● the fact of the promises of Scripture;
● the fact of our own confession of faith.

→ If some course members are to be baptised/confirmed/ received into membership, it can be pointed out that the affirmation of faith is made more objective by being made in front of the church.

Jesus promises not only to receive us if we come to him, but also to stay with us:
● 'I will come in...' (Revelation 3:20)
● 'I will never turn away anyone who comes to me.' (John 6:37)
● 'I will be with you always.' (Matthew 28:20)
● 'God has said, "I will never leave you; I will never abandon you." Let us be bold then and say, "The Lord is my helper, I will not be afraid. What can anyone do to me?"' (Hebrews 13:5–6)

→ Have small cards with Hebrews 13:5–6 written on them ready for each member. It can be suggested that they might learn the verses by heart.

This section should be ended with prayer, possibly based on this verse, in which you pray that each member may know the assurance of their faith as a sure foundation for their lives.

C Afterwards

What happens once we have become a Christian or been baptised in the Holy Spirit?

There will be difficulties

➔ A simple visual aid with 'Difficulties' on one side and 'Opportunities' on the other may drive home the two main points of this section.

After his baptism Jesus was 'full of the Holy Spirit, and was led by the Spirit into the desert where he was tempted' (Luke 4:1).

Do not regard opposition as necessarily evil – it may be the Spirit's way of establishing and strengthening our faith. However, make sure the members are prepared for:

- **Misunderstanding:** People who have not had the same experience will have difficulty in understanding what has happened to them. By all means speak about it, but be wise, especially at home where actions speak louder than words.

- **Guilt:** Sometimes things emerge from the past which again make us feel guilty, or we do something which makes us feel ashamed – indeed, under the tuition of the Holy Spirit our consciences may be more active.

  Encourage them to receive once again God's forgiveness and peace (1 John 1:8) – sin is not uncommon! However, remember that 'there is no condemnation now for those who live in union with Christ Jesus' (Romans 8:1).

➔ Course members sometimes feel excessively guilty because they have received so much from God and yet still lose their temper and so on. It may be reassuring to them if leaders confess a) that they themselves sin, and b) that after repentance they experience complete forgiveness and freedom through Christ.

- **Doubts:** We do not always feel as though we have become a Christian and been baptised in the Spirit, but that does not matter because we are resting on the facts of God not our emotions.

- **Difficulties:** Life does not always run smoothly and becoming a Christian does not assure us of an easy passage – on the contrary. However, we are given a new strength to deal with difficulties and they can be used constructively (James 1:2–5).

There will be opportunities

Since the Holy Spirit is not only given to us for personal help but so that we can be of service to others, we should not be surprised if opportunities come our way. If we put ourselves at the disposal of the Holy Spirit by a daily dedication to God, we will have a new ability to help others. We should not be frightened to trust God to work through us.

→ It is likely that members will already have experienced something of this. Draw out their experience and show how the gifts of the Spirit are already beginning to be manifest. It is frequently found that the gift of wisdom is the most usual, though often unrecognised, gift.

Next week we shall be thinking further about this when we look at the ministries God gives to the church and our place within them.

D Growth

Read John 15:1–10 and then think about it quietly for a couple of minutes. Encourage the group to share what strikes them as important from this passage.

→ This introduces what may for many be a new way of using the Bible and should not be rushed because of the unaccustomed silence.

Draw out the principles of growth.

If we are to remain useful to God and in close touch with him, we need to keep on growing. Healthy plants need a variety of nutrients (nitrogen, potash and so on) and the right surroundings (light, warmth and so on). A Christian needs prayer, sacraments, fellowship and support within a Christian church. (If you wish to drive this home put packets of fertiliser alongside a Bible, chalice and paten and jug of water on the floor or a table.)

God has provided means by which we
can receive his goodness and grow
closer to him. There are five basic
means and they are like the
spokes of a wheel – each one is
important if our Christian lives
are going to be the right shape
and travel smoothly.

→ It may be best to draw the outline beforehand (so that the circle
is circular) and write in the words
as you teach.
→ The teaching on the video may be
used at this point.

Prayer

Prayer needs to be cultivated if it is to remain alive. Different
patterns of prayer will be right at different times in our spiritual
lives, but there must be an overall discipline of prayer. We spend
time on those relationships we value – the time we spend in prayer
can be a monitor of how much we value our relationship with God.
However, beware of making too many rules about prayer – a child
does not make laws as to how and when it speaks to its parent.

→ Draw out from Christians in the group what their pattern of
prayer was in the past and how it has changed during the
course.

Praise is a very important part of our prayer life – by praising we
'get things in focus'. We praise God because of who he is, not
because we happen to feel like it. It is important to continue to use
the gift of tongues if God has given it to us – remember that it does
us good even if we do not understand it. Although frequently
it is a prayer of praise, tongues may also be used for confession or
intercession.

It is important to pray with other Christians as well as by ourselves
(see Matthew 18:19–20 and the church in Acts).

We should pray with other Christians at special meetings (explain
your local pattern of prayer meetings or house groups and so on),

but also we should seize other opportunities to pray when we happen to meet, for example over a cup of tea after shopping or when doing practical work round the church. Prayer should not be selfish. Although it is right to pray for ourselves, most of our prayer should point away from ourselves.

The sacraments

The classic definition of a sacrament is 'an outward and visible sign of an inward and spiritual grace'. Those on the course who have experienced conversion and baptism in the Spirit have received the 'inward and spiritual grace' of baptism and confirmation – and those who are not baptised/confirmed/received into membership should now publicly proclaim their faith in Christ and their membership of the church because these are the appropriate 'outward and visible signs'.

The regular receiving of holy communion is an essential part of the Christian life. (More teaching on the Eucharist will be given at the last session, if it is decided to adopt option 1 in Session 9.)

→ This section is not intended to be detailed teaching. It is important to ground what is said in the life and experience of your particular church, and it may be appropriate to give further teaching, and to tie in this section with their present experience of the sacraments. Be careful not to overbalance the session by giving too much teaching at this point. Individuals in the group will need further guidance after the session if they have not been baptised/confirmed/received into membership.

Bible reading

The Bible is one of the most important ways in which God speaks to us. Read 2 Timothy 3:16. Like prayer, there are many different ways of reading the Bible, but it is important that we have some sort of personal discipline. The link-work booklets have introduced two different methods, but there are many other ways, e.g. studying a character or theme, using a simple lectionary, following a system of daily Bible reading or studying with a commentary or other book.

➔ It is important not to go into too much detail at this stage –
above all, the importance of a daily habit should be
stressed. Explain that the link-work booklets finish at the end
of this week and introduce the members to any Bible
reading notes you think are appropriate for them. Give them
time to look at them, but it is probably best not to distribute
them until next week so that they finish the link-work. There
are now many different resources for Bible study and people
should be encouraged neither to get into a rut nor become
ill-disciplined. Persistence is important as well as variety.

Service and fellowship

These will be considered next week when we will be thinking
about ministry and the church.

E Prayer

Try to allow plenty of time for prayer and expect and encourage the
use of gifts. It can be particularly helpful at this stage to lead the
group in singing in the Spirit.

8 The church and us

Aim

◆ To teach about the importance of the church and of each member within it.

▶ Leading the session

This session marks a change of gear. So far the emphasis has been on the personal renewal of the individual. In these last two sessions members are encouraged to look away from themselves towards the world. There may well be a continuing need for personal ministry to some individuals within the group, but the group as a whole should now be encouraged to look outwards to their ministry in the church and the world. This cannot be covered in detail, but this session is intended to outline what God's purposes might be for them – it sets out a menu of possibilities.

In order to encourage this sense of personal responsibility for others, the session includes an opportunity for commitment to the local church. It has been found that members are prepared to take this with all seriousness, and the opportunity should not be missed, or presented as an optional extra. We should not sell the church short, or be apologetic about it. The benefits of Christian fellowship are so important that we are depriving people of something of great value if we hold back on this. Well before this session, thought should be given as to the possible ways of marking this commitment:

● It can be made within the group and marked by prayer for every member who wishes to make a commitment.

● It can be recognised by the whole church – some have written the promise in Section D in fine writing on parchment-like material and brought it forward at the main Sunday service, followed by prayer by the whole church.

● Others have made use of their written promise as an act of witness at a baptism/confirmation service.

By this time in the course members will know each other well, and be much freer in voicing their opinions. Encourage this and help people to listen and respond to each other rather than having everything addressed to the leaders. This in itself will help them to realise that Christian fellowship is not leader-dominated and each has something to bring – which is the message of Section B (it is also good preparation for whatever follows the end of the course).

At this point there is usually a realisation that the course will soon be over, and some uncertainties will be felt about what is to follow. Make crystal clear what the options are, and ensure that each person knows what he or she may do: if possible set it out in writing. It is therefore important that Section E is thoroughly thought through beforehand. There is often a real sense of disappointment that the course is ending and members should begin to become excited about what is to follow.

Session 9 is important in helping the changeover from this course to whatever is to follow. Two possibilities are suggested:

● To centre upon fellowship and thanksgiving with a shared meal and a communion service.

● To emphasise witness by throwing a 'party with a purpose'. Course members are encouraged to ask friends and relatives to a party at which the idea of a Saints Alive! group is explained and the newcomers are invited to become part of a new group (starting within two or three weeks).

A decision about which option is most appropriate for the group should have been made beforehand, and the necessary a dministrative arrangements made.

 # Timing

0-10 mins	Prayer and A Link-work
10-30	B The body of Christ
30-40	C Guidance
40-55	D The church member
55-70	E After the course (the video may be used)
70-85	F Prayer
85-90	G Administration

By this stage in the course the input of members is usually considerable and close timing becomes more difficult. However, the balance of the session should be kept. The tendency is for each section to take longer and for the last part to be rushed.

 # Presentation

Begin with a short time of prayer.

A Link-work

Are there any questions?

B The body of Christ

What has it meant to the members to be part of this group?

→ Spend some time discussing this. Have they learnt things in the group that they might not have learnt on their own? What have they learnt of the ways in which fellowship can be helped – and harmed? How can it be maintained?

When we become Christians we become part of a body – one of the pictures used in the New Testament to describe the church. It was the picture used by Paul in 1 Corinthians 12, the passage we read when we were thinking about the gifts of the Spirit. This session we are going to look at a similar passage in Romans.

Read Romans 12:4–13 and notice the following points:

● There are many different parts to a body (v. 4) – they all belong.
● Each part has its own job to do (v. 4). Use your own arms, eyes and so on to illustrate this.

- However, there is an essential unity in Christ (v. 5) which all Christians share simply because they are Christians. We may not like all our fellow Christians and would not necessarily choose them as friends, but they are family and as a family we are called to love one another.

- In verses 6–8 Paul uses a number of specific gifts as illustrations: prophecy, service, teaching and so on. Each Christian is called to make some specific contribution to the life of the church – this contribution is called their 'ministry'.

  While 'ministry' can be defined as 'a Christian acting in love towards another person', we find that in certain areas we are particularly gifted by God. We shall not necessarily discover this ministry immediately, and other Christians may be able to help us by telling us how they see God's gifts emerging in our lives.

→ Use the analogy of a school. When a pupil is eleven, they take all the subjects on the curriculum, but as they progress up the school they begin to specialise and take fewer and fewer subjects, but at greater depth. They need guidance to find the right subjects to take.

Explore this in the context of your particular church – consider some of the ministries which are being exercised. Do not make this too 'churchy': illustrate it by talking about ministries being used in the community and the world as well as those within the church. People should be encouraged wherever possible to 'have a go at anything' without fear of failing. Part of being the family of God is about allowing growth and experimentation in an atmosphere of loving support and acceptance.

- Whatever we are called to do, we should tackle it with determination and enthusiasm (vv. 6–8, 11).

- Notice again the importance of love and respect for our fellow Christians (vv. 9–10). Remember that love can be very practical (v. 13).

⊂ Guidance

→ Inevitably the question of 'How do I know what God wants me to do?' arises. This is a subject which requires more time than this session can give, but a beginning can be made by looking again at Romans 12.

Read Romans 12:1–2 and notice that verse 2 ends with the climax of the two verses: '...then you will be able to know the will of God'. So, in order to find out what God's will is, we must first:

- dedicate our lives to him (v. 1);
- not 'conform' to the 'standards of this world' (literally, 'be squashed into the mould'; v. 2);
- let God 'transform' our way of thinking (v. 2).

The will of God is often found not by lonely struggling by an individual, but by talking and praying with others. Note that Romans 12:1–2 is in the plural.

⊃ The church member

Talk about the importance of being fully involved in the local church.

→ It may be helpful to duplicate the following page (adapting it as necessary) and to hand it out to all members of the group. This is an important commitment and the paper should not be scruffy. A copy of it is included in the link-work booklet.

Go through the handout together. Help members to see that belonging to the church in this way is much more than a matter of giving. As we give of ourselves, so we receive (see Luke 6:37–38).

Members ought not to feel under pressure to sign this commitment. It may be best not to ask them to sign the paper at the session but to suggest that it is brought to the final session. They may well need to talk it over with their families.

I ....

**have decided before Christ that I will seek his help to
be a loyal member of**

....**Church.**

As a loyal member, I will:

◆ be regular in worship and prepare for it with care

◆ join with others for fellowship, prayer and study

◆ give care and practical help to those within and
outside the church, especially those in greatest
need

◆ give regular financial support

◆ exercise the gifts God has given to me

◆ pray for members of the church

◆ accept and support the leadership – not
unthinkingly, but as a responsible adult

◆ continue to think about my faith and how it
relates to my home, work, recreation and the other
parts of my life

◆ seek to share my faith with others (by praying for
them, looking for opportunities to talk to them and
inviting them into the fellowship).

Signed.. **Date** ....

🄴 After the course

How can we continue and build upon what we have received together as a group? What are our hopes and expectations as the course comes to an end? Lead into a discussion about the future and your own hopes for the group.

→ The testimonies in the video may be shown here.

🄵 Prayer

By now the group should be able to worship together freely. Spend time thanking God for one another and for all you have received as a group. Pray for the future and for the life of the local church. Once again, use music if possible and expect the gifts to be manifested.

🄶 Administration

- Hand out the Bible reading aids decided upon last session and explain the arrangements for Session 9.
- Whatever form you have decided that Session 9 should take, encourage participation by as many course members as possible.
- If Option 1 (a shared meal and communion) has been decided upon, work out a simple menu, decide the quantities of food required and invite course members to contribute particular items. Two or three can be asked to come early next session to help to lay it out. Explain that the communion service is fairly informal and for all members of the group. (Anglicans may note that while it is possible that some of the members may not yet be confirmed they will almost certainly, in the words of the *Book of Common Prayer*, 'be ready and desirous' of confirmation and so may receive.)
- If Option 2 (a party with a purpose) is your choice, arrange for the food and start praying for those who are to be invited. This evangelistic event needs to be carefully planned and course members need to feel completely involved. Because of numbers it may be necessary to change from the usual venue.

9 A party: communion or evangelism

 Aim

◆ To end the course with teaching and experience which is appropriate to the group.

 Leading the session

The way in which the course ends should depend on the needs of group members, the pattern of church life and the way the course has progressed.

Two models are given here in detail – one centres upon fellowship and the other on evangelism. There are other possibilities and churches have been known to have one of the following as an alternative to Session 9 (or in addition to it):

● A party to which family members are invited.

● A more formal Eucharist with a meal afterwards.

● A party for the whole church which course members organise.

● Some social or evangelistic outreach which the course does together.

The important elements seem to be:

● An encouragement to look outwards.

● An opportunity to act together. Group members need to be able to give their testimony and show that their new depth of faith has a practical application in helping others.

- An opportunity to wind up the course in a way which means that members are more excited about what is going to happen than mournful about leaving behind what has happened.
- Fun! Nearly all courses which have ended well have found that some sort of relaxed meal is of great benefit. Having fun together seems to be important.

 # Timing

Because of the many possible ways in which this session may evolve, it is impossible to give timing. However, once a programme has been decided, leaders will find it helpful to write down a timetable for the meeting. This is particularly important if there are those who aren't course members present.

> 'Good meetings are like football matches – 90 minutes with 30 minutes for extra time if it is needed.'

 # Presentation

Option 1: **Shared meal and Eucharist**
➜ The meal may precede or follow the Eucharist.

A *The shared meal*
Often it is best if this can be served in a room different from the one normally used for the meeting so that the usual room can be prepared for the Eucharist (although eating and worshipping in the same room may have symbolic value). The meal should be simply presented and served, without undue fuss, so that there can be a relaxed time of enjoying one another's company.

B *The Eucharist*
Look briefly at the word–prayer–meal structure, using the normal church prayer book.

The service should be creative and informal with as much participation as possible, though there is value in keeping the usual liturgical structure that they will find in church. The Scripture reading(s) can be read by member(s) of the group (some of John 6 is quite appropriate); the 'sermon' can be a sharing by group members of their insights on the chosen passage; and the intercessions can be extempore. The peace should be prolonged, with members encouraged to greet every other member of the group, and where your church discipline allows, the feeling of fellowship may be extended by each member administering the bread and wine to the person next to them, using their name.

A final word of exhortation on 'be filled with the Spirit' (Ephesians 5:18, literally, 'go on being filled') would be appropriate, emphasising that a constant infilling means a constant outpouring to the world.

Option 2: **Evangelistic 'party with a purpose'**
This needs to be carefully planned and executed, especially as new people will be present. It should be decided at the outset whether the purpose of the meeting is to be directly evangelistic or to encourage people to come on a new course. It has usually been found that the latter is best.

At Session 8 or earlier, course members should be asked to invite friends and relatives. (In some areas it may be helpful to produce special invitation cards and give them to members for distribution.)

Members should be asked to let leaders know the numbers they will be bringing. The venue should be large enough to accommodate them (but not too large), and it should be well prepared beforehand – course members should be asked to help in this.

Leaders themselves will wish to set an example by inviting people who have shown an interest in coming on a Saints Alive! course or are recent contacts, but the main responsibility for the invitations should rest on course members.

The meal should be organised as in Option 1, Section A, above. Course members should see themselves as the hosts and take responsibility for welcoming and entertaining the guests. It should not be too formal and should follow the normal social pattern for parties in the neighbourhood.

After the meal and a relaxed time for talking, a few members can be asked to say what the course has meant to them. This should not be too long – an interview technique where the leader or another member of the group asks questions can keep it within bounds. Lengthy testimonies are not suitable.

The leaders should then outline the nature of the course. Some of the material from the introductory meeting can be used. If so, another introductory meeting may not be necessary. A tentative date for the first session should be fixed. This should take place as soon as can be arranged.

In some groups, guests can be asked there and then if they wish to join a new course, while in others time should be given to enable them to think it over. Course members should be given responsibility for following up the people they brought.

Administration (following either option)

Make it absolutely clear what is happening next – if the group is continuing to meet, then when and where; if members are to join other groups, then who their link person will be; if there is to be no group support, then who is going to look after them.

Emphasise that they are not to be hesitant to approach you at any time for advice or help.

Make a date with each member for about three months' time so that you can see them privately, find out how things are going and encourage them on their Christian path.

Encourage them, if they have enjoyed the course, to recommend it to their friends. This does more than help you recruit new members – it helps them to begin to witness.

Send them on their way rejoicing!

Appendix

Baptism in the Holy Spirit – where does it fit into Christian initiation?

In the New Testament, Christian initiation (or becoming a Christian) has at least six discernible dimensions:

(a) **Repentance and faith** – the conscious turning from sin to God in response to the preaching of the cross (Mark 1:15; Acts 2:38; 3:19).

(b) **Baptism in water** (Acts 2:41; 10:47; Romans 6:3).

(c) **Anointing with the power and gifts of the Holy Spirit** (Acts 2:38; 10:44–48; 11:15–17; 1 Corinthians 12:4–11).

(d) **Acknowledging Jesus as Lord** (1 Corinthians 12:3; Romans 10:9; Philippians 2:11).

(e) **Joining the fellowship of believers** – the church (Acts 2:42–47; 1 Corinthians 12:12–13).

(f) **The knowledge of God as Creator and as Abba, Father** (Galatians 4:6) which in turn leads to a desire to express our love and thanksgiving in worship (Romans 8:15). Some would add here the assurance of forgiveness and justification (Romans 5:1; Ephesians 1:7).

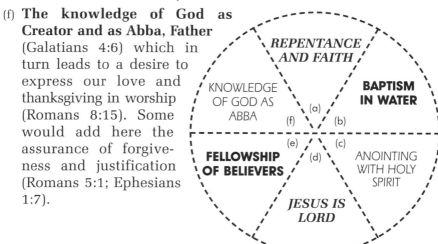

Thus we could say that our response to the grace of God shown to us in Christ is through:

- (a) and (d) – personal commitment
- (b) and (e) – corporate belonging
- (c) and (f) – openness to the Holy Spirit

The first can be said to underline the Protestant emphasis on personal response to God, the second the Catholic stress on the corporate nature of the church and the third the Pentecostal requirement for experience. Protestants often stress the work of God the Son, Catholics that of God the Father, and Pentecostals the action of God the Holy Spirit. It suggests we need the whole Trinity in full Christian initiation!

Different people enter into the Christian life through different segments. None is possible without the finished work of Christ and the prior working of the Holy Spirit in the individual and the church.

As will be clear from the references, these elements are inextricably interlinked (hence the dotted lines between the different segments of the diagram) and together form a whole. There will be differences of emphasis for different people, but these must never be allowed to destroy the unity of God's design:

Chronologically these six aspects may happen in any order. (One person is baptised as an infant, grows up in the fellowship of the church, comes to a personal relationship with Christ through repentance and faith as a young adult and begins to enter into the power of the Spirit in their thirties. Another may have a mighty experience of the power of God that only subsequently leads to church membership and baptism.)

Experientially one aspect may be far more significant than another. (Some people have a dramatic conversion, others experience a powerful baptism in the Holy Spirit, others find that the emphasis changes with the passing of time and the discovery of what for them are new truths.)

Theologically these different aspects belong together and perhaps one could say that Christian initiation is incomplete until a person has begun to enter into and appreciate all six. For many people the baptism or release of the Holy Spirit is the key that gives a deeper appreciation of all the rest.

This course has been written with the conviction that repentance and faith and the anointing with the power of the Holy Spirit belong together. Hence there is no deliberate attempt to lead people in a prayer of commitment at the end of Session 2, but ministry is reserved for Session 6. We are also convinced that the New Testament knows nothing of the lone Christian. The call to follow Christ is at the same time a call to join his disciples in the fellowship of the church which is explored in brief in Sessions 7 and 8.

In the course we use the phrase 'baptism in the Spirit' to talk about the anointing or release of the Holy Spirit with power in a person's life. We are aware that this does not necessarily accord with the way the phrase is used in the New Testament where it appears to refer more often to the totality of Christian initiation. However, where most of the church has for too long diminished this distinctive dimension of the work of the Spirit, we believe the phrase expresses something very important. If you choose to use some different terminology, be careful not to water down all that is implied in terms of surrendering to and being drenched by the mighty Spirit of the living God. For some the laying on of hands with prayer for the Holy Spirit in Session 6 will be a powerful and immediately life-transforming experience; for others it will be a quiet but no less significant opening up to God. For some there may be tears or laughter, tongues or prophecy; for others a deep assurance of God's presence and peace. God tailors our experiences of himself to meet our particular needs.

The approach taken in this appendix does not claim to answer all the theological questions surrounding baptism in the Holy Spirit. Our concern in writing this course is that people enter more fully into their inheritance in Christ and are empowered and gifted for his service in the world. Terminology is of secondary importance. Nevertheless, the model set out here is one which we believe reflects the complementary strands within the New Testament and has been found helpful to many people, and it is offered on that basis.

PERSONAL NOTES

PERSONAL NOTES

PERSONAL NOTES

PERSONAL NOTES

PERSONAL NOTES

PERSONAL NOTES

PERSONAL NOTES

PERSONAL NOTES

PERSONAL NOTES

PERSONAL NOTES

PERSONAL NOTES